The Relation Equation

The Relation Equation

_____

STEPHEN ROSENBERGER

RESOURCE *Publications* · Eugene, Oregon

THE RELATION EQUATION

Resource Publications
An Imprint of Wipf and Stock Publishers
199 W. 8th Ave., Suite 3
Eugene, OR 97401

www.wipfandstock.com

ISBN 13: 978–1-4982–0267-1

Manufactured in the U.S.A.   10/13/2014

The Relation Equation is dedicated to the diehard optimist who loves unconditionally and forgives perpetually; to the relationally challenged who fails and tries again; to the heartbroken, lonely, and hurting soul. The Relation Equation is written for you and me; the ones who fail to exercise perfect love in our relationships and must look to the heavens for an example to follow. In essence, The Relation Equation was written for all, and dedicated to all.

CONTENTS

PREFACE

Telling the story of behind the creation of The Relation Equation often creates more questions than it answers, but that is precisely how I prefer it. Building equity in a relationship initially seems ridiculous; at least, it did to me. As a matter of fact, I asked multiple people if my inner monologue regarding the topic was simply my own nonsensical way of processing ideas or if relationship equity truly had a wider audience.

The vast majority of experiences driving the text, some of which you will find overtly stated as examples within, occurred over a period of time spent with my cohorts (Tyler and Alyssa Bream) in Cleveland, Ohio, as we launched a faith-based, non-profit, community-oriented art gallery. Appropriately so, the gallery was named Agape, as the love of God was the primary reason for our presence there. Our operating model was centered on building relationships with the people of the community, be it artists, servers, restaurateurs, bartenders, shop keepers, educators or the average Joe resident.

As we began interacting with our community in early 2011, we immediately encountered difficulty with objectively describing, let alone quantifying, any success we had building relationships. The community we served was not an easy one to break into, which is a point mentioned later within the text. In fact, many a business failed to begin operations, or was significantly delayed, because of insufficient support at block-club meetings. We knew from the onset that building credibility with our neighbors was paramount to Agape's success and our ability to provide a viable service to a community we so very much loved. Through an intentional building of relationships, we sought to be trusted enough to serve our neighbors and used relationship equity to gauge whether or not we had sufficient credibility to do so.

The process of intentional relationship building continued through the departure of my original cohorts and the addition of an extraordinary young woman by the name of Laney. Laney came to Agape as an intern in mid-2013 and secured a full-time staff position within four months; the girl was incredibly talented. Her most apparent attribute was the unique ability to build and maintain relationships with practically everyone; no one felt left out so long as Laney was present. This one thing was certain: Regardless of whose voice represented our organization at any given time, the persisting objective was the formation and growth of meaningful relationships.

ACKNOWLEDGMENTS

To anyone and everyone who has poured into me: thank you from the bottom of my heart. I've often stated that there has never been a person I met who did not impact my life in some manner: so to all I have encountered in this life: thank you. My family and friends whose constant love and support motivates me to accomplish more today than I did yesterday: thank you. Colleagues along the way who inspired me to be better than in times before: thank you. Most of all I must acknowledge my Lord and Savior Jesus Christ: thank you!

Tyler and Alyssa Bream, you crazy kids bought into the idea that the missional life could be lived-out through a small art gallery in Cleveland, and you encouraged me to pursue the notion of relationship equity: thank you. Matt Anderson, you encouraged me to keep writing when I wanted to "punt my laptop out the window," and you came up with a fantastic name for this book when I simply could not: thanks man. Renee, thanks for letting me bend-your-ear about the business end of the writing process: you were a bigger help than you may know. Lorene, you're an example of how editor can be attentive to the mechanical problems in a piece of writing and led by the Holy Spirit with regards to content: thank you.

INTRODUCTION

It occurred to me a number of years ago that the concept of building equity in an asset had applications reaching far beyond the contexts of corporate and consumer finance. In fact, I worked with equity in the financial services world for a number of years before believing that additional applications were sensible enough to introduce to other individuals passionate about building relationships with those around them.

To varying extents, we all employ relationship equity but may never have defined it as such. By defining relationship equity, we challenge ourselves to be intentional about employing it, thereby leading a more effective life: be it with our families, coworkers, or friends. Whether you begin reading The Relation Equation as the CEO of a Fortune 500 company, a middle manager at a steel mill in a blue-collar town, or as a tireless laborer at an organization dear to you, the principles of relationship building universally apply.

The chapters to come will focus on what relationship equity is, so it seems appropriate to spend a moment informing the reader of what it is not. To the more cynical reader, although it may appear to be, it is not an attempt to create an all-encompassing formula to explain every nuance of relationships; I am simply not that wise. The principles found within this text apply to relationships universally; thus, the express purpose of the remaining pages is merely to reframe a well-known portion of the human experience with terms previously unused.

The Relation Equation is not a strategy to assist with the "use" of people for personal gain by appealing to their susceptibilities (i.e. getting on their good side): people are intelligent enough to detect when they are being manipulated or used. A healthy relationship requires pure motives, even if one does not approach this text with a subscription to the same westernized Christian worldview to which I, as the author, subscribe. Having stated such, each and every one of the arguments presented assumes this basic construct: The foundation of relationship must be love.

In the chapters to come, you will be challenged to wrestle with theories and methodologies that may occasionally seem cold and formulaic, but stick with it. Understand that these are not attempts to diminish a supernatural influence upon relationships; in fact, my hope is that you will find the biblical model of building relationships amply useful toward informing the process of restarting broken relationships, and mending breaking ones.

Happy reading!

1

EQUITY

Prior to launching into an explanation of what relationship equity is, it would be beneficial to address the definition of equity. The Relation Equation is not written in order to provide a complete understanding of the mechanics of equity, as it is not a technical manual designed to offer such. Even so, my desire is that following chapter 1 you will be able to sufficiently apply the concept of equity to the paradigm of relationship building. There are plenty of other resources better suited to providing a holistic explanation of equity as it applies to the accounting of tangible assets. Having stated such, equity is a term that the vast majority of adults will encounter at some point in their lives–whether as a consumer or as a business professional. Given our purposes, a simplified definition of equity is this: Equity is the remaining claim after all outstanding liabilities are subtracted from the present value of an asset. The term Equity will assume only a positive value for our purposes, as negative equity in the context of relationships will be periodically referred to as strain (S).

Consider a hypothetical scenario in which I sell my home, presently valued at $200,000. In this example, let's say I still owe $100,000 from the first mortgage when the house was initially purchased and an additional $25,000 from a home equity loan I took out a couple of years ago. The total amount owed on the house is $125,000–I am liable for repayment on that amount; it is not mine. What is mine is the difference between the appraised value of the home and the sum of the liabilities, which is $75,000, more commonly referred to as owner's equity.

WHAT EQUITY DOES

Equity in an asset is contingent upon several factors. Although the list of determinates of an asset's value is significant and relative to the type of asset being evaluated, we will narrow our focus to three general factors that I feel to be most important to our cause. These factors are the present appraised value, the investment made by the investor or investors, and any outstanding liabilities against the asset.

Appraised Value–Equity is contingent upon the present appraised value of the asset at any given point in time, as assigned by one empowered to offer such a valuation. Note that there are two crucial elements within the definition: (1) The appraised value is based on the present value of an asset, not a previous value. This is not to say that understanding previous values lacks validity; in fact, it provides sound information regarding the stability of the investment. (2) The appraisal must be completed by someone qualified to offer such information. Typically, this is done by an experienced, well-credentialed, and unbiased third party. Note that the third party appraisal process is subjective, based on well-informed opinion. An individual who is negotiating acquisition of an asset may not agree with its appraised value, determining it is not of the same value to him/her as it is to the appraiser. Assignment of value is a personal decision.

The appraised value is assigned initially by several factors and can change based on those same factors over time. In this section our focus will turn to these four variables that affect appraisal value, including: (1) the condition of the asset, (2) comparable assets, (3) the conditions under which the appraisal is being requested, and (4) the physical location and attributes of the asset. This is not a comprehensive list, but a list of factors most relevant to understanding application of equity to the relationship paradigm.

(1) The appraised value is invariably linked to the condition of an asset. The inescapable reality is that contemporary western society assigns worth based largely upon present condition. Consider the purchase of a rusted, beat-up vehicle whose engine starts only when the temperature rises above fifty degrees. Without knowing much else, it would be easy to conclude that this vehicle may not offer the reliability needed, especially if it commands a high price. The condition of the asset has much to do with its valuation.

During my short stint employed in the mortgage industry, I vividly recall viewing appraisals of rapidly deteriorating homes. Even in a professional environment, I began experiencing empathy for the inhabitants living in less desirable residences. Still, as prescribed at the bottom of the appraisal's page 2, the licensed appraiser assigned a well-informed, yet subjective value to the residence in question.

Another example is the recent surge in viewership of television shows that catalog the reality of home improvement and renovation, especially those that empower the growing population of homeowners known as do-it-yourselfers. There is one particular show that dares to call home rehabilitation an addiction. The show's ambitious host knows that restoring homes to their former glory is an investment in the home's value and thus an endeavor to create additional equity in the asset. If the condition of the asset is disrepair, the primary concern becomes the amount of resources (both time and money) required to repair the asset. As in the case of the flipped house, the investor must perform a detailed cost-benefit analysis to determine if the amount of investment required for repair, in addition to the cost of acquiring the asset, will remain less than the forecasted resale value.

(2) The appraised value is contingent upon comparable assets, more commonly referred to within the industry as comparables. A comparable asset should embody characteristics similar

to those of the subject asset whose value is being sought. Although comparables may not be direct replicas of the subject asset, an examination of their collective, fundamental attributes ought to reveal more commonalities than differences. Consider a comparison between a flawless 2-karat diamond and discolored 1-karat cubic zirconia. They are both stones, but that is about the extent of their similarities; they are not comparable assets. However, if the flawless 2-karat diamond was compared against another flawless 2-karat diamond, it could be said that the primary attributes of the second diamond are similar enough for the stone to be called a comparable.

Determining the value of comparables helps establish a sense of the demand for the asset. Is the asset desirable to others who are looking to acquire it? Essentially, one could have invested greatly in an asset and yielded no sellable value if there were not a buyer willing to exchange liquidity for the asset. A non-liquid asset is worth the present appraised value only if someone (a buyer) determines that it warrants an exchange of his/her liquidity for it. The housing bubble/market crash of 2006 in the United States is a prime example of this, as it brought to light over-inflation of property values. Many homeowners were stuck with subprime mortgages they could not afford and homes they could not sell resulting from the negative equity.

Consider a different type of asset. Picture a man of aging years, bound primarily to his home because of his failing health. After repeatedly seeing the same infomercial for commemorative coins, he decides to make both a hobby and investment out of collecting them. Although these collections hold value, mass-production makes them easy to acquire; thus, there is very little present demand for resale.

(3) The value of an asset is based upon the conditions under which it is being assessed. Although conditions may not apply in every occurrence of valuation, they can occur if some form of distress is present within the ownership of the asset. A common example would be financial distress of the owner. If the liabilities are not being paid as initially agreed upon, the asset will likely be

repossessed by the lienholder, as in a foreclosed residential home. In many cases, the original loan amount extended by the bank far exceeds the market value; thus, when the bank forecloses and re-sells the property, it takes a loss.

Consider the impact of situational conditions upon value in terms of personal settlements. If I have recently lost my job and am unable to pay the rent this month, I may be inclined to sell my tangible assets for less than their market value. In that moment, maintaining a residence for my family is of far greater importance than securing the best possible offer for the sale. Note: In this par-ticular scenario, there are both needs-based as well as emotional drivers at work to alter my valuation of the assets.

(4) The appraised value of an asset is dependent upon its physical location and visible attributes. This factor considers any unique characteristics about the asset, even external ones, in terms of its physical situation/location or the view/vantage point that it has. In keeping with our example of residential home appraisals, most of us can point to certain areas of our respective hometowns that offer a unique physical characteristic, such as a central down-town location, an unobstructed view of a well-known landmark, or exceptional community benefits, as in the case of a cooperative. It is no mystery that properties with these additional attributes typically come with a higher price tag than similarly situated assets without them.

I have always envisioned one day living in a penthouse apart-ment overlooking the Manhattan skyline, as have many others. Although the price of such an abode is significant, it offers luxuri-ous living, appealing views, and uncanny proximity to nearly every amenity known to man (or so it seems). Given the limited supply and high demand for a property offering such unique character-istics, the appraised value of the asset will be greatly affected by its physical location and visible attributes. As we proceed further in the text, I would encourage you to recall the methods that we use to value tangible assets, as those methods equally apply to our valuation of relationships.

Investment–Equity is contingent upon the investment made by the investor, whether initially, over a period of time, or a combination of both. The initial investment in the asset can be thought of as a down payment. Consider an asset that is yet to be acquired. You desire to assume ownership of it but are unable to immediately pay the full asking price. However, you are able to pay a percentage of it now and remit the remaining payments over a period of time. The asset has a presently appraised value of X; and, for our purposes, we will assume that the price tag for acquiring the asset is also X. Since the price tag and the appraised value of the asset are equal, any investment made at the onset equates to immediate equity, or claim, in that asset.

I remember having my first legitimate car-buying experience at the age of twenty-two. Until that time, I purchased lemons with what little money I earned from part-time jobs during high school and college, combined with the financial assistance of family. However, graduating college brought a turning point to my life, as I would be off to graduate school shortly and would need a car that didn't require me to replace leaking oil as much as I filled up with gas. Although I was more financially stable than in prior years, I certainly did not have the necessary cash to purchase a more reliable vehicle outright. The compromise requested by the bank was that I invest a sum of money now (the down payment) and make regular monthly payments over the course of the next three years.

The agreement to acquire an asset for which you cannot immediately pay in full stipulates the aforementioned down payment but also is requiring of periodic payments to satisfy the remaining liability. As payments are applied toward the outstanding liability (the margin between the initial price tag and the down payment), liability decreases and equity increases. Of course, this assumes the appraised value remains steady or increases from the appraised value at the time of asset acquisition.

Liabilities–Equity is subject to any outstanding liabilities against the asset. This particular concept will be addressed in greater detail in the next chapter, with specific application to the relationship paradigm. Earlier, we concluded that periodic payments can cause an increase in equity provided the appraised value remains stable. In many cases, though, there may be several liabilities (or liens) against the asset. A common example of this would be a homeowner who has taken multiple lines of credit out against the equity in his/her home. Whether the asset has several or a single lien against it, the lien holders must be the first parties to be reconciled upon sale of the asset and done so in the order of primacy in which they had previously negotiated.

Stating that equity is subject to any outstanding liabilities on the asset is similar to stating that the amount of money that you have is dependent upon, in part, the amount of money that you have spent. In broader terms, I am unable to possess that which I have exchanged for something else. This nuance of equity applies to situations where an individual exchanges the entirety or a portion of his/her ownership in the asset for something else.

WHAT EQUITY DOES

The practicality and reach of equity is immeasurable. Anyone who has owned any percentage of an asset at any time has engaged in equity. Given that even the poorest and most downtrodden of society have possessed something material at one time or another, owner's equity becomes a universal experience. The paradigm of equity offers a concrete form with which to establish ownership, create a standard of accountability, and provide a measure of stability and transition into liquidity under certain previously indicated circumstances.

Ownership–Equity (in the form of owner's equity) establishes ownership of an asset and holds the owner or owners accountable for its care. As aforementioned, in order to have equity in an asset, one must have some sort of recognizable ownership of it. It is impossible to hold equity in an asset to which you have no valid claim. The claim implies responsibility, and the owners become stewards of their asset. For example, when I purchased my first vehicle, the down payment signified my contractual obligation to care for it. Given such, when parts no longer functioned properly, it was my responsibility to have them replaced; I was the vehicle's steward.

Assets that lack good stewards have a much greater risk of depreciating in value; and, when an asset depreciates in value, equity is negatively affected. In essence, stewards become caretakers of the asset through assuming the responsibility of maintaining or increasing its value where possible. I am reminded of a phrase well known in the medical community that you may recognize as a sentiment of the Hippocratic Oath: "First do no harm." Stewardship makes no allowances for occurrences of neglect.

As a result of stewardship, stabilizing and further increasing the amount of equity is a burden that falls primarily upon the primary owner rather than upon any other party. It may seem unfair that the margin of owner's equity is more significantly affected by ebbs and flows in valuation rather than by lien holders occupying the margin of liability. Consider that the lien is attached to the asset with predetermined repayment terms that are independent of changes in value over time. The risk involved for the lien holder is based on the stability, ability, and willingness of the investor to satisfy the long-term obligation successfully, while the owner's investment is a risk based on the valuation of the asset at any given point in time. For example, if I am a poor steward of my first legitimate vehicle and neglect necessary repairs, the value of the asset, and my owner's equity in it, will subsequently decrease. Regardless of ebbs and flows in valuation, my obligation to repay the lien holder based on the original agreement remains unchanged.

Liquidity–Equity can transition into liquidity; however, this is greatly contingent upon a buyer being found for the non-liquid asset. Someone must be willing to exchange liquidity for it. A common example would be an individual consumer attempting to sell his/her primary asset, a home. Once the asset is sold for an agreed-upon price (somewhere near the present appraised value unless other conditions are present) and all outstanding liabilities against the asset are paid (i.e. any home equity lines of credit or liens), then what remains is the owner's equity. At this point, owner's equity is returned to the owner as liquidity.

A second example of transition to liquidity would be an individual consumer seeking out a home equity line of credit on his/her home. The challenge in this scenario is locating a lender willing to exchange temporary liquidity for an additional lien against the asset. In this model, the owner of the asset is merely borrowing against the equity in the asset for the sake of temporarily using liquidity.

Stability–Equity can provide a measure of security and stability to those who exercise stewardship over it. As an investment, net-positive owner's equity in an asset has potential value. In addition, the owner's claim affords him/her permission to utilize whatever benefits the asset naturally provides. For example, owner's equity in a home allows the owner to reside in the home while payments are being made toward the outstanding liabilities against the asset.

Whether or not we can immediately access the liquidity of an asset, its very presence offers a sense of security. Simply knowing that I have acquired an asset of some value gives me an indication that, even if I lost my ability to gain further equity, I am not destitute. This principle is without scale. Consider an individual who has found himself/herself on the street, without a home. The very few possessions that he/she may be holding become quite dear to him/her.

Armed now with a baseline understanding of equity, the journey of applying equity to the paradigm of relationships may begin. In chapter 2, you will be introduced to the construct of relationship equity and the relation equation.

2

RELATIONSHIP EQUITY

Having increased our understanding of equity and valuation, we can apply these concepts to relationship maintenance. Committing to this task requires shifting from the assumption that relationship maintenance is a random, thoughtless process to accepting the premise that relationships may grow, remain stable, or decline as a result of human action. Connecting the components of equity calculation with their corresponding components in the relation equation requires a thorough investigation of their dependence upon and reactivity to one another.

The fundamental assumption moving forward is that the relationship is the asset. However, the relationship does not demand the presence of anything tangible, as a relationship is an entirely intangible series of emotional exchanges.

The relation equation will include these four intangible components: Relationship Equity (E), Relationship Strain (S), the Potential Value of a relationship (P), and a breakpoint that we will introduce as the Tolerance Threshold (T). The formula itself (Appendix B-1) determines relationship equity (E) by subtracting the relationship strain (S) from the tolerance threshold (T).

Since the potential value (P) of the relationship is limitless, it is restricted only by the parties involved in the relationship. Inasmuch as the potential value (P) is limitless, it will always exceed the value of relationship equity (E), relationship strain (S), and the tolerance threshold (T). Simply put, the potential value of a relationship is the relationship's optimal state. The contention moving forward is that, if love is infinite and the basis of relationship is love, then the potential value of a relationship is also by association infinite and never fully attainable; similar to perfection, it is impossible to attain fully.

RELATIONSHIP EQUITY (E)

In terms of the chapter 1 discussion on equity, relationship equity would most closely mirror owner's equity. It is best expressed as the expendable portion of a relationship's potential value and is the margin in the relation equation that represents ownership through periodic or lump sum investments by one or more of the involved parties in the relationship. There are, of course, other variables that can alter the value of relationship equity.

Take, for example, a relationship with two participants, John and Jane. The amount of relationship equity, or the expendable portion of the relationship for John to use, is dependent upon his investment in Jane. Likewise, the amount of relationship equity, or expendable portion of the relationship for Jane to use, is dependent upon her investment in John (Appendix B-2). To each one of us, this means that investment in a relationship will yield positive equity.

The expendable portion of the relationship for John is dependent upon Jane's tolerance threshold, and the expendable portion of the relationship for Jane is dependent upon John's tolerance threshold. Factoring in the tolerance threshold addresses the reality that, regardless of the significance of John's investment in his relationship with Jane, the value of the relationship cannot exceed Jane's tolerance threshold. This single nuance of the relation equation explains many of our relationship challenges.

As I began reflecting upon my own relationships, it became apparent that this is an identifiable phenomenon in every human interaction that I have. Whether I am the primary investor in the relationship, subject to the limitations set by the other individual (or vice versa), my investment in another is worth only what he/she determines it is worth. In cases when investments are not valued by the intended recipient, they are still validated. The adage that "no good deed goes unnoticed" is accurate if we accept that God accounts for our otherwise unrecognized good deeds.

Proceeding through the balance of the chapter, the relationship between the components within the equation will become more evident. For ease of calculating the value of relationship equity (E), it was presented above so that it could be easily related to the components below:

RELATIONSHIP STRAIN (S)

If the relationship equity is the asset, then relationship strain (S) represents all of the outstanding liabilities against the asset. In a balanced relationship, there are ebbs and flows in the amount of relationship equity; these do not put the relationship into strain or count as outstanding liabilities because they are similar to using some owner's equity and then replacing it. However, when withdrawals are made that use up more than the equity that has been invested, the result is that any withdrawal is taken from depleted equity; it is damaging to a relationship and should be classified as relationship strain (S). The forms of relationship strain (S) are: unrepaid withdrawals, unreconciled infractions, transferred infractions, and unearned relationship value.

Unrepaid withdrawals– Consider a hypothetical scenario in which my employer has given me five paid personal days to use at my discretion during my first year of employment with the company. I begin my new job in early February and take a five-day vacation to Seattle in late September. As a man of 33 years, I am relatively healthy and cannot foresee any need to take additional time off between now and the end of the year. However, this year the flu virus is especially vigorous, and I find myself in need of calling in sick two days in mid-December. Whether or not my employer elects to compensate me during my time away due to illness, I have exceeded the allotted number of days off granted to me at the beginning of the year; the relationship with my employer is in a state of strain. Chances are, if I am a salaried employee working on time-sensitive projects, I may need to reconcile any unrepaid withdrawals by putting in extra hours at the office to make up for the ones missed due to illness.

Unreconciled infractions–Unreconciled infractions are offenses against the relationship that have gone without reparation. This is not a reference to unforgiven infractions, since the biblical model of handling relationships requires unconditional forgiveness of wrongdoing. An unreconciled infraction is a reference to offenses against the relationship that resulted in equity depletion, but no (or insufficient) equity has replaced the loss.

An unreconciled infraction can occur through a direct offense between relationship participants or by relationship association. In the case of the direct offense, the offense occurs against the other individual in the relationship (i.e. John offends Jane, or vice versa). Although we may be quick to forgive, forgetting the infraction becomes the real challenge. In an instance of an unreconciled infraction, there is a looming knowledge of a debt owed by the person who wronged the other one.

Take for example an all-too-common scenario in today's society in which an individual's husband or wife has committed an act of infidelity; he/she has cheated. After the infraction has been exposed, the offended participant in the relationship is required to offer forgiveness to the offender; however, the wounds of the offense may remain and serve as a persisting reminder of the pain inflicted by the offender. Furthermore, depending upon the offended one's tolerance threshold (T), the relationship may not have sufficient equity and margin of strain to sustain such a blow; this is why many relationships dissolve following such an offense.

Consider a different scenario in which a business partner behaves unprofessionally toward the company's largest client, causing them to take their business elsewhere. Although the business partner is apologetic and immediately forgiven, equity in the partnership has been negatively affected by the infraction that was committed. At this point, the business partner can choose either to maintain the status quo (unreconciled infraction) or to remedy the situation by replacing the lost business with new clients (reconciled infraction).

Transferred infractions–The following account is of a man named Arthur, a resident local to the neighborhood in which the gallery was situated. In fact, Agape was the first space in which Arthur displayed his wall art; and he did so proudly–he was an advocate of his work and our organization. Arthur would often stop by the gallery, usually while on his way to a sporting event or benefit. We would chat about many topics–politics, art, religion–but the one thing Arthur usually ended up discussing with us was his recent dating woes.

A couple of years prior to our arrival in Tremont, Arthur's wife passed away. He found the dating scene especially daunting later in life, often citing the hesitancies of prospective women to trust again. Despite his best efforts to convey his own trustworthiness, he had been repeatedly unable to overcome the barrier of trust projected upon him by women who had previously endured failed relationships with untrustworthy men. In Arthur's case, although he was not the individual who had infracted against the women in past relationships, by association of his gender he assumed the relationship strain (S) between the women he dated and their previous partners.

Unearned relationship value–Accounting for unearned relationship value is both challenging and subjective. Unrepaid withdrawals and unreconciled infractions speak to "having relationship equity and losing relationship equity" while unearned relationship value speaks to the relationship equity that could have been attained but never was. This does not imply, however, that relationship participants should cease striving to achieve a perfect relationship through perfect love.

Historically, the best example of perfect love was stated when Jesus declared (Appendix A-1) that the ultimate act of love involves sacrificing one's own life for another. In one declaration, He both foreshadowed the unmatchable act of love that He was soon to complete through His death on the cross as well as prescribed the necessary attributes for His disciples to embody in order to appropriately reflect such perfect love.

Dangers of Strain (S)

When a relationship has encountered strain, where one party is indebted, liable, or trapped in a state of negative equity, the risk of relationship dissolution is greater.

If the damage done to a relationship has been too significant, a relationship participant with negative equity could be thrust closer to the tolerance threshold. In essence, a strained relationship should be perceived as potentially volatile because there are consequences to continuous withdrawals upon the potential value in a relationship once the relationship equity has been depleted. Although there are a number of possible consequences, only the loss of trust, loss of the ability to be heard, and simple resentment will be addressed.

Loss of Trust–Arguably, an obvious consequence of withdrawing from a relationship in a state of strain is loss of trust. Similar to the way that consistent withdrawals on a line of credit make a consumer risky to a lender, so also do consistent withdrawals against a relationship (in a state of strain) present a risk to the other participant in the relationship. Trust is predicated upon historical action, present resources, and future potential.

In my late twenties/early thirties, I held a job in consumer finance that required me to perform risk analysis on unsecured lines of credit. The institution that employed me engaged in two controversial risk mitigating activities. The first activity was a reduction of credit lines to ensure further withdrawals could not occur until a portion of the existing indebtedness was repaid. This action did not end the relationship; it merely lowered the tolerance threshold

(T) to just above the present point of strain (S). The second activity was a more controversial closing of accounts. This action lowered the tolerance threshold (T) to a place below the present point of strain (S), thereby ending the relationship. In this scenario, the lender (the one both literally and figuratively withdrawn upon) has given up on the relationship. Although the lender is essentially hoping for repayment of the outstanding debt, termination of the relationship will likely provide necessary closure, even if full repayment is not received. Satisfaction comes in the simple knowledge that the debt cannot increase and that the debting behavior will cease.

No Longer Heard–As a leader, losing the ability to be heard is a calamity. Primacy is placed on this over "loss of trust" because trust implies that you will deliver on your word. However, if you have lost the ability to be heard, trust becomes a non-factor.

Politicians who have spent any time in office have experienced this. Many times campaign promises are offered with good intentions; not every politician speaks maliciously, despite popular belief, although for whatever reason their promises do not always come to fruition. These accumulating failed promises serve as relationship infractions against the populous that voted him/her into office, and future promises have a greater propensity to fall on deaf ears.

In some relationships, as in that between parents and their estranged teenager, losing the ability to be heard may be based on perception over fact. Consider a scenario in which a parent forbids the teenage child from attending a friend's party at which there will be no adult supervision. Based on his/her own experiences and risk analysis, the parent determines that allowing the teenager to attend the party presents a safety concern. As a result, the teenager perceives the parent's decision as detrimental to his/her social status. Since the teenager places greater importance on social status than on potential safety concerns, he/she declines to trust the judgment of present and future parental decisions and may not request parental permission in the future; the parent is no longer heard.

Simple Resentment–The third potential danger of strain is the pervasiveness of simple resentment towards the offender in the relationship. The party in the relationship negatively affected by withdrawals may or may not continue to extend relational activities based on a sense of obligation, pity, or the influence of second-degree relationships. Withdrawals permitted under strain may result in resentment.

During the process of writing this text, I have been forced to evaluate my own relationships in a way similar to that I hope you are compelled to do now. The truth is that I am not always entirely impressed by my own motives. There are many seemingly good deeds that I have committed, which may appear noble to an outside observer, but which have been laced with my own resentment from start to completion.

Jesus spoke emphatically about the connection between attitude and action. As a result, those who share a Christian worldview understand that actions performed out of resentment are of no positive, eternal significance. It is my personal summation that if an action cannot be carried out in love, it should not be carried out at all.

Strain and Equilibrium–If one relationship participant has negative equity and the other relationship participant assigns greater value to the relationship, then negative equity or strain is moved closer to a state of equity equilibrium. Consider a scenario in which Jane has significantly indebted her relationship with John, thereby inviting a state of strain. However, what might happen if a number of John's other relationships began to deteriorate, causing him to place more value on his remaining relationships, such as his relationship with Jane? Although the amount of strain has not decreased as a result of equity-building activities, it has decreased because John has assigned a greater potential value to the relationship. In doing so, John has moved the relationship closer to equilibrium and further away from the tolerance threshold (T) or breaking point of the relationship.

Strenuous Extensions

Most of us can identify one or more persons in our lives with whom we have engaged in a relationship despite their continued withdrawals. If this allowance happened as a result of charity, the reasoning would be socially justifiable as our perspective would mirror that of Christ. In such cases, withdrawals are subtracted from an extension of granted positive equity (E), not perceived as a strain.

Charitable Allowances–Whether or not your worldview mirrors that of my own, the idea of extending charitable equity for a greater purpose is a universal part of the human experience; I choose to believe there is a bit of "good" in everyone who desires to do "good" for his/her fellow man. In the biblical model, Jesus (Appendix A-2) likens performing charitable actions for one another to doing so for Him. Regardless of the level of strain (S) upon the relationship, when charitable equity is involved, the withdrawals become externalized. What does this mean? For me, it implies that the withdrawals against the relationship come out of God's infinite bank of equity as opposed to my finite supply. What I can tolerate (T) and what God can manage are for obvious reasons very different. Subsequently, withdrawals made under these conditions, even if the relationship was already in a state of strain, require the prescribed alternative treatment of an extension of positive equity (E).

Consider the work performed at a local homeless shelter. Week after week you tirelessly serve the very same people, listening to the gut-wrenching stories that led them to a life on the streets. Your compassion to serve allows frequent withdrawals from those less fortunate, which inevitably becomes emotionally taxing. Although your heart breaks, the numerous withdrawals seemingly do not create strain between you and those whom you serve.

The concept of charitable allowances can apply to any relationship founded on service, regardless of compensation. Over the past number of years, I have had the pleasure of building meaningful friendships with some of the teachers and professional staff of a primary school in urban Cleveland, Ohio. The dedication they exhibit to return to work day after day is uncanny given the obstacles awaiting them. Amidst seas of underprivileged children functioning at varied levels of ability, the dedicated few give of their time and resources, often to see only minimal results. Despite the children's unintentional propensity to continuously withdraw, the educators are able to tap into an unlimited source of equity. Whether or not they would attribute the limitless source to God's infinite bank of equity, I do.

Second-degree Relationships–Charitable instances aside, there are cases in which we may continue allowing withdrawals on a strained relationship if second-degree relationships are involved. A common second-degree relationship would be familial; maybe a family member through marriage whom you are socially obligated to assist as a result of association. Take, for example, the step parent of an adult child who is addicted to a controlled substance. The biological parent is likely involved regardless of infraction magnitude or frequency, although the step parent may elect only to involve himself/herself because of his/her association with the biological parent.

Allowing continued withdrawals in a second-degree relationship is not limited to one's family. Consider attending the wedding of a couple whom you do not know. The invitation comes from a close friend's request to accompany him/her as his/her date. You attend the wedding as a favor to your friend, although you have no vested interest in the couple getting married.

Hopeful Optimism–This particular strenuous extension permits withdrawals amidst the state of strain (S) because an individual feels as though the infracting person's behaviors will eventually change. I am fairly confident that most other pastors or counselors would willingly attest to the predictable session in which a relationship participant is involved in a toxic relationship but believes that his/her partner is on the verge of a life-altering transformation. As a result, the participant in the relationship who is absorbing the infractions continues doing so.

Consider a physically or emotionally abusive relationship. In this scenario, one dominant participant intentionally issues infractions against the relationship via physical or emotional force with the purpose of creating a wound. Although this behavior is socially unacceptable, the offender attempts to acquire equity from the other participant in the relationship through force. Following consistent withdrawals via this negative behavior, the abused participant in the relationship sometimes grows increasingly attached to the negatively behaving participant in something mirroring Stockholm Syndrome (identifying and sympathizing with the offender). Furthermore, in permitting such withdrawals, the infracted-upon participant lies to those with whom he/she has good relationships so as not to appear connected with someone who is not equally invested in the relationship. Unfortunately, these lies can in and of themselves become infractions against the victim's healthy relationships because it breaks those bonds of trust.

Dysfunctional romantic interactions tend to be breeding grounds for hopeful optimism and the compounding lies that often accompany it. Consider a woman who invites a man into her life with whom she has no present or future prospects. She works two jobs to pay the rent, the car notes for both of their vehicles, and assumedly picks up the tab for nearly everything else. She bears these arduous burdens while her boyfriend spends his day playing video games, eating Funyuns, and drinking light beer. Visualize this guy placing his game on pause the moment she walks in the door just to check if she brought him enough crispy fried onion snacks and Bud light to replenish what he plowed through earlier that day. All the while, she defends his actions to those on the outside, even if it necessitates lying about how the bills are paid.

Although this misguided young woman knows that this particular relationship is a toxic one, she continues to make attempts to salvage it for the sake of appearances. Any chance that the landscape will change appears dismal to any onlooker who has been made privy to the whole story, but that does not stop her from perpetuating the lie to herself that the situation will change and presenting a false depiction of their lives to others. Her hopeful optimism may compel her to protect the relationship and the guy involved, but this strategy will prove only to cultivate loss of trust in her other relationships.

POTENTIAL VALUE (P)

The third and fourth components of the relation equation, potential value (P) and tolerance threshold (T) are linked together as indicated at the beginning of the chapter. Simply put, the potential value of a relationship is the relationship's optimal state. If love is infinite and the basis of relationship is love, then the potential value of a relationship is also by association infinite and never fully attainable, similar to perfection, it is impossible to attain fully. The potential value of a relationship exists only as an infinite value only so long as the tolerance threshold has not yet been breached. Once the tolerance threshold has been breached, the potential value (P) of a relationship is equal to zero. Note that the individual responsible for setting this value can change as either participant's tolerance threshold increases or decreases.

Restated, when the tolerance threshold adjusts, so does the potential value because the potential value of a relationship is limited only by the constraints of those involved. Consider a couple, John and Jane, who have agreed to begin dating, or possibly recall your own experience in doing so. Initially, there is hesitancy to fully trust or to be completely vulnerable before the other person; but, as you begin to grow in the knowledge of his/her revealed character, barriers against trust and vulnerability begin to fall. As the couple's tolerance for one another increases, the potential value of the relationship also increases.

TOLERANCE THRESHOLD (T)

Every participant within a given relationship has a tolerance threshold, the point at which the relationship has lost potential value to him/her and has reached its ultimate breaking point. The tolerance threshold (T) cannot be a fixed value, because it must be free to change with an individual's decision of when to terminate a relationship. Inasmuch as the tolerance threshold (T) changes, so also does the potential value (P) of a relationship. Although a relationship's potential value (P) must always be greater than its tolerance threshold (T) (if allowed the potential value (P) would be infinite), the potential value of a relationship is limited only by the tolerance threshold (T) placed on the relationship by the parties involved. Only in perfect love can the tolerance threshold (T) ever equal the potential value (P) of a relationship.

Let's revisit John and Jane's dating relationship described in the previous section. Assume, for our purposes, that a month into dating Jane discovers that John has been married and divorced three times in the past five years. Even though a month of dating has allotted enough time for some equity to be built in the relationship, the omission of such significant information constitutes an irreconcilable breach of trust. Jane can no longer tolerate any additional infractions against the relatively new relationship and therefore perceives no potential value in a continued relationship with John.

In chapter 1, we discussed the mechanics of equity and established a baseline understanding of it. As we transitioned into chapter 2, the Relation Equation was introduced, and the process of connecting elements of equity with corresponding components in the equation began. Now, as we proceed into chapters 3 through 5, we will develop a better understanding of how equity is gained or lost.

3

BUILDING EQUITY

Now that we have devoted great time and effort to defining equity and applying the concept to the paradigm of relationship, we may begin to unearth practical applications of how we may begin to acquire this intangible asset. In chapter 3, you will be introduced to the process by which relationship equity is granted as well as earned. Following a discussion on the methods by which earning and granting occur, we will evaluate the component building blocks of positive equity.

GRANTED EQUITY

A primary method of acquiring equity is through the granting of it–often accomplished through a down payment on the asset, which for our purposes is the relationship. The benefit of offering a portion of ourselves at the onset is that it provides immediate equity. A person gives away some of himself/herself when committing to a relationship with another individual regardless of whether or not the relationship is familial, platonic, or romantic. By offering this down payment, relationship participants allow themselves to become mutually vulnerable, which means open to both the desirable as well as unwanted potential outcomes. As in the case of all other types of investments, some element of risk, calculated or not, is involved. Still, without risk there is no potential for reward.

Virtue of the Office–One way that equity can be granted is by virtue of the relationship or office (i.e. a teacher or a physician) a person holds or newly acquires. He/She is granted equity up front, even before he/she has had an opportunity to earn equity. Essentially, the people or organization that he/she commits to serve offers a down payment on the relationship with the expectation that he/she will perform the prescribed functions equitably.

A broader example of granted equity by virtue of the office is civil authority. Those in government, regardless of one's voting preference or approval of his/her decision-making ability, are endowed with the authority to govern the masses. A certain amount of relationship equity is allotted by virtue of the office at his/her installation. This societal reality may be unpalatable for many (and historically has proven to be) because, as opposed to voluntary submission, granted equity by virtue of the office demands involuntary submission; and western society unenthusiastically embraces being told what to do.

Another example of equity granted in this manner is that of pastoral leadership. On my first Sunday serving as the Assistant Pastor at Alger Assembly of God, I was immediately received by a loving church that placed significant value in the pastoral office. Although I spent a great deal of time working to earn equity at the church in the years following, the congregation granted me a substantial amount of equity upon arrival. They did so prior to knowing the extent of my trustworthiness or willingness to be vulnerable before them.

Unlike civil authority, an individual can choose to leave a religious community with relative ease should they disagree with the leader's choice of direction. However, if the congregation opts to submit to the leadership of a pastor, there is a certain amount of relationship equity that is granted at the point of installation into office. Although the relationship between spiritual leader and parishioner begins with granted equity by virtue of the office, it has a tendency to become subject to the same dynamics of other at-will relationships. This is not to diminish the continued authority of a spiritual leader granted by the office, but to say that the relationship transitions into a more intimate one through the parishioner's willingness to be vulnerable.

Virtue of the Relationship–There are three ways in which equity may be granted via virtue of the relationship. They are dependence, submission, and association.

A common example of relationship equity being granted because of a dependent relationship is that of a parent and child. In most instances, the love a parent has for a young child is immeasurable; thus, the tolerance threshold (T) a parent has for the child's behavior approaches nearer to an infinite potential value (P) than it may with any of his/her other relationships. The sentiment is reciprocated by the child's complete dependence upon the parent for sustenance. The biblical model (Appendix A-3) describes a child's duty to obey the instruction of his/her parent, as well as the parent's charge to act within the child's best interest.

A second way that equity may be granted by virtue of a relationship is through voluntary submission. Consider a marriage relationship as depicted by the biblical model (Appendix A-4), prescribing a mutual, voluntary submission between husband and wife. Both participants in the relationship agree to invest in the needs and desires of the other by relinquishing their own. In essence, his/her interests become secondary to the spouse's.

A third way in which equity can be granted is through relationship association. Take, for example, an existing relationship between John and Jane, as well as an existing relationship between Jane and Alex. John may receive granted equity from Alex because of the pre-existing equity that Jane has with Alex or vice versa. This is a classic "I'm with him" or "I'm with her" scenario in which positive relationship equity is granted to participants through a shared relationship.

EARNED EQUITY

Based on observation alone, earned equity is the most common and likely way for relationship equity to increase. Whether or not we consciously put forth the effort to build equity, we do this on a regular basis. Consider the vast majority of homeowners in the United States; they cannot afford to purchase a residential home with the liquid assets they have saved in their bank accounts. Instead, they form an agreement with a lender to make consistent principal (and interest) payments, most traditionally over the course of ten, fifteen, twenty, or thirty years. As payments are remitted, the principal portion of that payment decreases the amount of the outstanding liability against the asset, thereby increasing equity (provided, of course, that no other conditions have been altered). The same is true of the vast majority of relationships; they are built through consistent deposits.

Relationships are typically built over a period of time. This is not to say that newly formed relationships cannot have significant equity, for we have already addressed the value of granted relationship equity. More often than not, time is a vital element in the composition of a relationship that is built and solidified through a battery of shared experiences. Consider, for example, a young boy and young girl who grow up next door to one another, all the while becoming childhood friends. At an early age, they watched the family from the other end of the quaint cul-de-sac bring home a baby; and they learned about life. They were in class together when word came from the school principal that their second grade teacher passed away, and they learned about death. In their teen years, they became one another's first kiss; and they learned about love.

Sharing experiences is more significant than merely recalling the same event; it is about processing exposure to common worldview components. The two kids did more than observe events together; they learned about life, death, and love through similarly situated conditions, which is the stuff of worldview soup. Worldview soup is a concept based on the primacy of nurture over nature, which I have taught on a number of occasions to undergraduate students. The simplified premise of worldview soup is that everything a person is exposed to in this life dynamically collects in a large bowl to inform who he/she is and what his/her conclusion regarding truth is. Whether or not two individuals who are exposed to similar ingredients of worldview soup opt to draw the same conclusion regarding truth is irrelevant to our presentation of relationship equity, as we have likely made our own observations that opposites can attract. What is relevant is that individuals exposed to similar worldview components, inclusive of shared experiences, are better positioned to engage in and build equity in a relationship over time.

COMPONENTS OF EQUITY

Through gestures or acts of great significance, equity can exponentially increase in a relationship; this reaffirms that all activities rendering an increase or decrease in equity are not of equal value. Furthermore, the value of an activity is independent of any monetary value; it is, instead, subject to the personal valuation made by the recipient of the activity as to whether it is positive or negative. Earlier in the text, the assertion was made that the value of an asset is contingent upon the value that a buyer assigns to it; therefore, the value of a gesture is worth only what the recipient participant in the relationship assigns to it.

Consider the difference between your neighbor's asking for a cup of brown sugar to complete his/her favorite cookie recipe versus a request for your help next Saturday with pouring concrete for a new driveway. Clearly, offering a cup of sugar from your pantry is the gesture requiring far less personal investment of time and resources. Given such, the assumption would be that the act of offering sugar would hold less value than the act of pouring concrete next Saturday. However, what if you offered your last cup of critical brown sugar after all the stores were closed on the night before the tri-state cookie bake-off? Suddenly, the intrinsic value of offering sugar has changed; and the offering of sugar has become more significant than the pouring of concrete. The value of the gesture flexes as the recipient assigns new value to it.

Any increase in earned equity is the result of relationship building, so it would be worth a concerted effort to investigate the primary components of relationship building. Although there may be many identifiable secondary components important to a participant in a relationship, those at the primary level fall into these two categories: trust acquisition and mutual vulnerability. Given the significance of trust in a relationship, more time will be devoted to developing an understanding of its makeup and implications.

Trust Acquisition–Trust is formed based upon historical action, present resources, and future potential. A record of historical action recalls the behaviors of the past specific to an individual's ability to perform relationship activities in a reliable manner. This discussion will not include the qualification of big promises over small ones, implied promises versus overtly stated ones, or fulfilled promises with good outcomes as opposed to fulfilled promises with poor outcomes. Each of those comparisons could independently warrant a complete text and are deeply subjective. The assumption we will use moving forward is that fulfilled promises equate to positive equity and promises broken equate to infractions against equity.

Imagery of this exchange often appears in films depicting a child of a divorced home awaiting the arrival of his/her other parent for the alternate-weekend visitation. In these grossly stereotypical scenes, the non-primary parent has a propensity to be neglectful of his/her duties to spend time with his/her child and opts for a more exciting personal venture instead. At this point the child is visibly disappointed in his/her parent; a relationship infraction has occurred, the result being a decrease in relationship equity. Contrarily, if the non-primary parent arrives as scheduled, the child's trust is not broken; in fact, the non-primary parent's reliability and equity increase.

Inasmuch as a historical record indicates past behavior, an account of present resources references a participant's ability to deliver on a promise now. However, given a time-sensitive situation where no prior history of a person's reliability is known, decisions of whether or not to trust are based on known or perceived present resources at the recipient's immediate disposal. When immediate delivery of a promise is required, the necessary resources should be expended for the purpose of fulfilling that promise immediately. Expediency of delivery is the result of minimal allowable time elapsing between issuance of and fulfillment of the said promise. Take, for example, a common retail transaction. At the point of sale in a retail store, the customer is required to remit payment for merchandise prior to taking possession of it.

If fulfillment of the promise is set to occur over time as opposed to immediately, then the question of present resources applies only to that segment that is required to be fulfilled now. In instances where delivery of the promise begins immediately and continues over time, resources should be expended for the necessary down payment, while sufficient potential resources for future fulfillment should be verifiable. Consider again the purchase of a residential home via means of a traditional mortgage loan. In a traditional loan, the purchaser is likely paying cash for a small percentage of the home's overall price tag. The remaining amount to be financed (paid over a specified period of time) is approved by a lender who confirms verifiable means for continued payments over the agreed upon term of the loan. The lender is evaluating the borrower's ability to maintain payments over the term of the loan based on historical action, the present financial situation, and a well-informed forecast of the borrower's future resources. Unlike verifiable historical action or present resources, determining future potential relies on some form of calculated risk assessment or action based on a more subjective gut instinct.

Risk assessment is the objective way to execute decisions in a relationship. This form of analysis considers data that, in the context of relationships, is based almost entirely on observation. Despite the seemingly subjective nature of individual data from observation, the collection process is balanced by those in close circles around us who offer their own observations of the potential relationship and its risks. Take, for example, observations from a relationship between John and Jane. Since John and Jane are each engaged in a relationship with Alex, Alex may be able to offer unbiased observational data regarding the relationship between John and Jane.

During one of my favorite pastoral activities, premarital counseling, I delighted in wearing these two observational hats: (1) playing the unbiased third party looking in on the future bride and groom's relationship, and (2) instilling the value in each of them to become a devoted observer of the other's blind spots. Note: Understanding my leadership in a typical premarital counseling session requires acceptance of the very atypical pastor that I am.

While playing the unbiased third party, I utilize a survey-based system that asks one hundred or so identical questions of both the future bride and the future groom. The basic questions are repeated and arranged strategically to increase the likelihood of honest answers, and the results are frequently significant. Once I have the opportunity to categorize and compare the answers, these blind spots become apparent: those areas of life that have been previously overlooked by starry-eyed puppy love. The illumination and reconciliation of key differences in innate desires between the two, at this point, serves to prevent greater relationship carnage at a later date when blind spots are discovered at inopportune moments in life.

The second part of counseling on blind spots comes from this personal ideal: a husband ought to be aware of his wife's blind spots; and a wife, aware of her husband's. Let's face it, guys; the majority of us functioning in the business world would give critical presentations and well-attended talks with crooked neckties, mismatched shoes, and lint-covered suit coats had the women in our lives not intervened, whether they might be wives, girlfriends, or concerned colleagues. Fashion faux pas provides a simplistic example of blind-spot awareness. You ought to know, ladies, that your contribution to the lives of men far exceeds prevention of wardrobe blunders.

Persons with strong family, friend, or collegial networks would agree that "blind spots" exist in spaces of our relational interactions; and our close circles have sight of them even when we do not. In essence, people gravitate toward those who will occasionally ride in the passenger seat with us and catch what our forward-looking glass (windshield) or historical record (rear view mirror) alone does not. With data consisting of observations from additional angles, we can more accurately perform risk assessment; this is one reason why references are required through so many life processes, including finding employment. Take, for example, a hiring manager: an organizational member required to methodically and consistently execute this particular process. He/She is presented with multiple applicants for a single open position. The risk of hiring an under-qualified applicant presents itself through the potential of his/her being unable to fulfill the necessary job requirements, while the risk of hiring an over-qualified applicant occurs because the applicant may immediately leave once a better offer comes along. In either case, the hiring manager must perform some form of risk analysis to determine which candidate would be the best fit for a long-term relationship.

When risk analysis fails to yield viable results, or when the results do not situate one option in a place of greater risk aversion, then the use of gut instinct is the preferred way to execute decisions in a relationship. Despite its inherent subjectivity, this form of decision making requires a reliable intuition and is subject to a battery of emotional drivers. Consider, again, the applicants interviewing with our hiring manager. Although their observable qualities may not grant either one of them an overwhelming advantage over the other prospective candidate, the manager may offer the job to one of them based on intuition.

An effective leader understands the value of potential possibilities and exercises wisdom when deciding which candidate will be chosen. Although risk assessment may provide answers that are logical or reasonable, logic and reason are not in-and-of themselves reliable as being wholly deterministic in the greater decision-making paradigm, especially as it pertains to the formation and maintenance of relationships. Having stated such, the most effective leaders know when to "throw the book out the window."

When the two paradigms work in concert with one another, gut instinct can serve as a tiebreaker when the risk assessment yields minimal definable direction. For example, if candidates for a job are similarly situated based on observable qualities, gut instinct can effectively serve as a tiebreaker. In the context of a dating or romantic relationship, we tend to utilize gut instinct over risk assessment during our initial interactions with the prospective mate. Although we would most likely refer to it as chemistry, gut instinct can grant one initial access into the relationship while risk assessment solidifies the bond. Conversely, for those who approach romantic relationships from an exclusively reason-based orientation, risk assessment can serve to narrow the field of potentially undesirable partners, while gut instinct is employed to select from the remaining population of desirable candidates.

Mutual Vulnerability–On the heels of trust is the building block of mutual vulnerability. Relationship implies taking a calculated risk while knowing that you may be hurt by the other participant in the relationship. Despite any potential risks, mutual vulnerability is a required component for any relationship's equity to increase.

A common complaint in romantic relationships, and an occasional reason for their dissolving, is that of a participant feeling that the other participant is "not letting them in" close enough. There is a reason why this is inherently destructive to a relationship. A lack of mutual vulnerability means these two things: There is no exchange of positive equity, and there is a consistent battery of infractions against the relationship. Since there is a party who appears to have lost interest (the one who is not expressing vulnerability), the participant who is attempting to be vulnerable may lower his/her tolerance threshold, thereby lowering the potential value of the relationship.

In chapter 3 we began the discussion on acquiring equity and uncovered its primary components. Now, as we proceed into chapter 4, we will explore the occasions when the equity that has been acquired in a relationship is used.

4

USING EQUITY

On every balance sheet assets are listed on one side, and liabilities are listed as part of the other side. Until now, our exploration of equity has focused primarily on the mechanics that add equity to a relationship. In chapter 4, the focus turns to events that subtract equity from a relationship.

VOLUNTARY USES OF EQUITY

In chapter 3, we outlined the process by which equity is earned in a relationship. Although we should not approach our relationships with the express purpose of building an account of equity to spend at our every whim, there are occasions when voluntary expenditures of equity are appropriate. Later in the text, the motives propelling voluntary uses of equity will be addressed; but for now we will simply attempt to develop a baseline understanding of voluntary uses of equity in a relationship.

In the course of living, each of us needs to eventually employ the assistance of another individual. As stated in the introduction, this is not a hard and fast formula to manipulate someone or appeal to their good sensibilities. Because we care about someone with whom we have a relationship, we sometimes exchange favors. I began telling a particular joke during my years at seminary about something that came to be known in my circle of friends as "moving credit." As one of us moved from place to place, corporate help with the labor was requested. Such moving credit assumes that, since someone previously helped me with a move, it is necessary for me to reciprocate in kind with him/her. There is a certain obligatory element involved in a scenario such as moving; however, the primary impetus for reciprocation is based upon a mutual understanding of standard relationship protocol. By engaging in relationship, a participant commits to some degree of consideration for another's needs and worldview.

The voluntary use of equity applied to the paradigm of leadership is especially relevant when requesting a participant's consideration of a new or controversial idea. In a position of leadership, some of the equity has already been granted by virtue of the office at the onset of the leader/led relationship, although the leader must continue to build sufficient credibility with a led person to obtain his/her buy-in on an idea or process that may vary from standard operating procedures. In many cases, organizations must alter trajectories to remain relevant to their markets, and redirecting requires the buy-in of their members. Buy-in, as opposed to mere submission or obedience, embraces the potential for innovation during the transition of processes; it is the difference between advances in a free market and a closed one. Within a free market, improvement upon an existing process is encouraged through trial and error, whereas a closed market punishes failed attempts. The benefit of leading with member buy-in is his/her vested ownership in the success of the process and willingness to innovate without fear of reproach. However, any attempt by a leader to gain member buy-in is contingent upon sufficient available equity for the voluntary use.

Voluntary uses of equity in leadership may, at times, involve more than the immediate members being served. In cases where the organization needs to restructure due to tightening financial constraints, a company may be forced to use drastic measures like mandatory staff reductions. Although they may be able to reduce a portion of the workforce through options like early retirement, this rarely rectifies the entirety of the crisis; and layoffs or firings are still necessary. Boards of Directors from publicly traded companies are forced to answer to shareholders, while smaller family-owned corporations face goodwill issues when impeding the livelihood of entire families in small towns. In either instance, the buy-in of the affected and surrounding community members is helpful in easing the inevitable impact on lives and easing acceptance of the transition if there is equity present to voluntarily be spent.

INVOLUNTARY USES OF EQUITY

Accidents–The most common involuntary use of equity is the occasional accident requiring forgiveness from the infracted upon relationship participant. A number of years ago, while I was still in my late teens, I was employed by a local distribution warehouse that shipped orders of adhesive products all across the country. It was a second-shift job that I would work with a few of my friends after my freshman-year college classes. On one particular evening towards the eleven o'clock end of our shift, I, a new forklift operator, was assisting my friend Shaun with a load that he could not reach alone. That evening Shaun got more than help. For the benefit of those who may not know, forklifts are assembled with a significant counter weight in the rear to balance out the heavy loads picked up from the front. Accidentally, I ran over Shaun's foot with one of the rear wheels of the forklift. Once the pain subsided, Shaun was okay and thankful that he had no broken bones. Even so, I made a mistake and required forgiveness from my friend.

There was plenty of equity in the relationship to sustain the mistake, but it was an equity withdrawal nonetheless. Even given the historical record of this instance and the fact that I had no further forklift incidents with him, I assume that, despite his willingness to offer me forgiveness, he still would be hesitant to approach a forklift that I was operating. Disclaimer: This does not suggest that offering forgiveness should be exclusive to those participating in an established relationship because unconditional forgiveness is a mandatory component of life.

The biblical model references an interaction between Jesus and the apostle Peter (Appendix A-5) as Peter attempts to develop his understanding of the extent of forgiveness we are required to offer those who have infracted upon us. In the initial directive, Jesus provides an exponentially greater boundary to forgivable offenses than Peter does in order to illustrate the limitless number of times we are to forgive an individual for a repeated offense. Jesus proceeds to indicate that the repetition of forgiveness is necessary because each one of us has already been forgiven more than we could ever forgive. However, in His typical fashion, Jesus chooses to use a parable to solidify the message. In the following verses, He tells the story of three men affected by debt. The protagonist of the parable owed a significant debt to the king; in fact, Jesus makes it clear that the debt was insurmountable. Given the exceptional breadth of what was owed, the servant was unable to remit payment for the debt. When faced with the dire consequences of payment default, the servant pleads with his master for more time to gather resources for payment; however given the enormity of the debt this promise was entirely empty. The text reads that out of pity the king (master) forgives the debt of the servant and later discovers that the servant has called in the debt of someone who owed him significantly less than that for which he just received forgiveness. As a result, the king (master) retracts his grand gesture of debt forgiveness and has the wicked servant jailed until the debt is reconciled.

The implication of this parable is quite simple: The forgiveness we offer to one another must be limitless, specifically in light of the forgiveness of sin offered to us through Christ Jesus. Mankind's sin is the unpayable debt requiring the grand gesture of forgiveness from the master. Although forgiveness of the debt liberates the one indebted, it equally frees the one who is owed from holding onto the debt any longer.

Vulnerability Event–Another instance of involuntarily withdrawing on the equity in a relationship is through a vulnerability event, which is a time of uncontrolled emotional turmoil. There are vulnerability-event scenarios in which equity is expended through receiving consolation for a traumatic life event such as the death of a loved one or other relationship dissolution. The relationship between John and Jane is being evaluated for the effects of involuntary equity withdrawal. In this case, we are not evaluating the effects of either John's or Jane's separating from their relationship with one another; we are evaluating the effect of Alex's separating from his relationship with either John or Jane. If John is required to cope with the death of a loved one, for example Alex, Jane would have an obligation to provide John with consolation, regardless of whether or not Jane and Alex had any form of relationship. This principle is not exclusive to death of loved ones; it applies equally to scenarios such as dissolution of marriages or other relationships of significant commitment.

There are also vulnerability-event scenarios in which equity is expended through efforts to intervene. For example, let's say a relationship participant requires someone to whom he/she becomes accountable or is confessing a life-controlling addiction. In these moments, regardless of whether or not the affliction or predicament was self-inflicted, the individual faced with a vulnerability event requires the assistance of those in relationship with him/her whether he/she is able to request it or not. It is, therefore, the responsibility of participants in relationship with him/her to recognize this need for an involuntary use of equity.

In chapter 4, we opened the discussion to uses of relationship equity and uncovered the manner in which it is used. Now, as we proceed into chapter 5, we will explore practical ways to maintain healthy equity in a relationship.

5

STABILIZING EQUITY

In the film business, reference is made to the meet-cute or moment when two characters meet (often with romantic implications) under entertaining circumstances. This is not news to any of us, though; we live a series of meet-cutes in our typical workaday lives. My Christian worldview frames these meetings as divine encounters; however, you may call them results of fate or destiny. In any case, we call them appointed meetings regardless of verbiage. So, if meeting is not the primary challenge, then what is? The answer to the question is maintaining equity.

MUTUAL EXCHANGE OF EQUITY

In the process of maintaining relationship equity, there must be a consistent and balanced exchange. Through a mutual exchange of equity, there are minimized significant net losses of equity; and the relationship does not approach relationship strain (S). This is accomplished through adhering to the processes earlier prescribed in the section in chapter 3 on earned equity. For example, when a mutual exchange occurs, John may be making withdrawals for himself; however, he is still pouring into the life of Jane through the cyclical process of mutual exchange. Thus, John's equity inflow becomes Jane's equity outflow, and Jane's equity inflow becomes John's equity outflow.

Consider the mutual exchange of equity that occurs during the holiday season in a romantic relationship. In this example, we will say that John and Jane are newlyweds, each with a number of Christmas parties that he/she is expected to attend. John's outflow of equity turns into Jane's inflow of equity when they attend Jane's family parties. In a similar manner, Jane's outflow of equity turns into John's inflow of equity when they attend John's family parties. The overall exchange of equity between the two is balanced, leaving neither party indebted to the other as a result of Christmas party attendance. Now if John makes an off-color joke about his mother-in-law's roast turkey being too dry, he's on his own.

This manner of mutual exchange parallels one of the most common, understated processes on earth: respiration. Although there are additional by-products in the reaction, the essence of our respiration is an exchange involving our intake of oxygen and expulsion of carbon dioxide. Conversely, plants use the carbon dioxide we expel, and give off oxygen. Members of the animal kingdom and plant kingdom engage in a mutual exchange that is critical to one another's survival.

RESTORING LOST EQUITY

Until now, our focus has been devoted to the causes for the net gains and losses of equity in a relationship. Although restoration of lost equity is a critical component to relationship maintenance, more is involved in the process than simple gains covering losses. There are three general scenarios in which lost equity needs to be restored, although the prescribed treatment should be different for each.

In the first of the three scenarios, the loss of equity has not exceeded the equity ceiling of one or both participants and therefore has not caused permanent damage to the relationship. The relationship is not broken or in a state of strain. Since relationship equity is still present, exchanges of equity are completed with relative ease and fall within the parameters of mutual exchange. This scenario is most commonly found in well-maintained relationships and is often taken for granted by those enjoying extended periods of relationship stability.

In the second scenario, equity loss has exceeded the equity ceiling but has not reached the tolerance threshold. Damage has been done to the relationship, but it is not necessarily permanent, provided infractions against the relationship cease. Although the relationship has entered a state of strain, it has not yet reached the tolerance threshold of either participant. The most evident and controllable solution is for the infracting participant in the relationship to cease the voluntary withdrawals. At the point of strain, voluntary withdrawals in a relationship are want-based and involuntary withdrawals are need-based. Furthermore, it would be necessary to address the reason for the involuntary withdrawals in an attempt to minimize them.

A prime example of the second scenario can be readily found in personal finance amidst crisis. When money becomes tight in a household, the remaining resources must be allocated for needs and not wants. If the net value of the wants exceeds the net value of what is being borrowed, then voluntary withdrawals, wants, must be eliminated completely. Furthermore, at the point of financial strain, a household must evaluate where cuts in expenditures can be made to minimize future voluntary withdrawals.

In the third scenario, equity loss has exceeded the tolerance threshold, and the relationship is broken. Essentially, this question could be rephrased as: "How do I mend a broken relationship?" or "Can I mend a broken relationship?" It is the contention of the relation equation that, once the tolerance threshold (T) has been breached, there is no longer a viable relationship remaining to mend. However, this is not an ultimate end to any possibility for the same relationship participants to reengage in an exchange of equity.

The relation equation simply demands that the relationship be returned to its most primitive state; it must go back to square one. Once the tolerance threshold (T) has been breached, reverting to the organic, primitive state is the only option. At this point, one or more of the participants in the relationship have determined that the relationship no longer has potential value (P) to him/her. In this particular scenario, the tolerance threshold (T) has been breached, which is the most catastrophic event possible in this model. Consequently, had there been an opportunity for the relationship to be mended, one of the two prior scenarios would have applied at an earlier time.

The aforementioned is predicated on the willingness of the same participants agreeing to enter a new equity exchange with one another. For example, a relationship participant may forgive his/her fiancé for an act of infidelity but still wishes to call off the wedding. In this scenario, at least one relationship participant does not wish to continue in an equity exchange, so the relationship is not presently salvageable. It may seem easy enough to conclude that the faithful participant would be hesitant to reengage in relationship with the one who committed the act of infidelity. The benefit of applying the relation equation to this all-too-common event is the development of an understanding that any hesitancy to reengage in an exchange of relationship equity is a result of breaching the tolerance threshold (T).

In cases where the relationship must restart from square one, additional caveats become prevalent. More stringent terms for reengagement will likely apply, since, although forgiveness has transpired, forgetting is a much more challenging endeavor. Naturally, the participant infracted upon will be a bit more guarded and require sufficient processing time before trusting and becoming mutually vulnerable again. Contrary to the desires and supplications of the participant in the relationship whose infraction caused the breach, restoration to the last functional point in the relationship is improbable. Relationships are not mechanical and cannot be treated as such.

The new exchange of relationship equity is requiring of a new down payment. In the chapter 3 discussions on granted equity, we determined that:

> A person gives away some of himself/herself when committing to a relationship with another individual regardless of whether or not the relationship is familial, platonic, or romantic. By offering this down payment, relationship participants allow themselves to become mutually vulnerable, which means open to both the desirable as well as unwanted potential outcomes.

Trust and vulnerability are especially significant because of an understandably greater risk of entering a similar relationship. Since the tolerance threshold (T) has already been breached once, investing in a relationship with a participant who has already breached the tolerance threshold is riskier the second time. Thus, any new investment in the exchange of relationship equity must be significant; it must be potentially greater than the first time around.

Take for instance the examples of loan default and residential home foreclosure. We had mentioned that relationship terms during the second attempt may be more stringent. This thought process parallels a lender's assessment of a consumer's credit history prior to granting a loan. In my first years working in consumer finance, underwriting for a certain partially secured product was a viable option for those who, for all intents and purposes, could not be trusted with a traditional unsecured line of credit. The consumer would offer cash collateral for up to 100 percent of the credit line for the course of a year. If he/she successfully managed to handle the credit line, the collateral was released to him/her and the line was converted to a traditional line of credit. In a similar fashion, a large down payment may be required on the second-time relationship because of the relationship history as opposed to credit history. Furthermore, access to the full benefits of equity exchange in a relationship may be limited until sufficient trust is reestablished and confidence is restored in an individual's ability to once again safely exercise vulnerability.

REINVENTING SELF

In all of our relationships, a pattern is set that provides the other participant with an expectation of what behavior is to come; in essence, our previous behaviors stand as indicators of our future behaviors. This statement does not provide a new or revelatory insight into human behavior; we have adopted this as normative whether or not we consciously consider our own thought processes about those with whom we have engaged in relationships. The idea of consistent behavior pervades almost every aspect of society, whether it is from song lyrics stating: "You can count on me" or the ever famous words of Popeye, "I y'am what I y'am."

Admittedly, I am not a fan of this premise, as it does not naturally promote the potential for change. Still, there are times in life when we evaluate our behaviors and make the determination that something needs to be altered. Usually, this comes as a result of disliking the present way that we are being perceived by those around us, particularly those with whom we are in relationship. Bear in mind that we are not speaking of superficial changes here such as attempts to lose those ten extra pounds, stop smoking, or even making the effort to spend more time with our wife and children. We are talking about a complete reinvention of self.

Making the decision to change is often the simplest part of the process; executing the actions that will lead to authentic change can be much more daunting. Moreover, convincing those engaged in relationship with you that the change in behavior is authentic could very well be even more challenging than the actual execution of the change. The primary question becomes whether or not you should reinvent 'self' in your present environment amongst those who might rigorously question the authenticity of your change or whether you should give in to the temptation to reinvent elsewhere.

Reinventing Locally–Reinventing in your present environment, or locally, will undoubtedly require evidence of changed behavior over a period of time. If you recall from our discussion on uses of equity in chapter 4, the prescription for applying forgiveness is boundless, as we have individually been forgiven much more than we could ever forgive. However, my suspicion is that, although we speak of a grace that wields enough power to forgive, we are hesitant to accept the premise that other persons can change (especially those who have relationally infracted upon us) until we are provided with substantial evidence to authenticate the declared internal change of behavior. Simplified, we will believe it when we see it.

While in the process of writing this book, I had the pleasure of meeting a woman named Anita, founder of Unchained Love. Anita experienced a particularly significant transformation, one that she was not hesitant to share with others, including me. Although I now interact with a thoughtful, relationally-minded, and faith-driven professional, Anita describes how the landscape of her earlier years greatly contrasted with the present view.

At an early age, relationships were difficult for Anita. Instability at home, combined with a barrage of physical and emotional abuses, left her desirous of a relationship that promised to withstand the tumultuous moments of this life. Instead, in her search, she found substance abuse and addiction to sex, inevitably leading to a lifestyle as a drug dealer and an escort. To say the least, the relationships that she was forming were toxic, based on a combination of codependence and transaction.

When Anita's life dramatically changed and the process of reinventing "self" began, she elected to do so locally. Committed to providing a good life for her baby boy, Anita sought refuge in the only option for a truly stable relationship: one formed with Christ Jesus. It mattered not what relationships once failed; Anita was determined to construct healthy ones moving forward.

Although Anita knew that her internal change was authentic, reconciling previous infractions presented a brand new set of challenges. Her pursuit of forgiveness was a given; she asked those whom she had wronged to forgive her in addition to offering forgiveness to those who had infracted against her. Even so, the expected caveat of the reconciliation process was a periodic unwillingness of others to accept her claim of a major life transformation. Anita understood that the consequences of previously infracted upon relationships were resulting in certain individuals' unwillingness to further participate in relationship with her. Furthermore, she found that the relationships that she had formed during participation in a toxic lifestyle had become endangered; those individuals now knew that Anita was unwilling to participate in the very activities that once united them.

The challenges facing Anita are normative for many who opt to reinvent locally following a perceived need for internal change. As indicated in chapter 4, the primary responsibility is a reciprocal issuance of forgiveness for any and all prior infractions against the relationship. Bear in mind, receipt of forgiveness does not automatically entitle a participant to a new investment of equity. Realistically, there are those who will genuinely forgive, yet be unable to reenter an exchange of equity with an individual who once infracted upon them. It is possible that, over time, the internal change will have become sufficiently apparent externally that an individual's hesitancy to reengage in an exchange of equity will diminish. Still, despite best efforts to amend, some wounds do not heal for some people.

Reinventing Elsewhere–We have already stated that convincing others of an internal change could be more daunting than executing one. Given the choice, it is arguably easier to relocate and reinvent elsewhere than to face one's past as Anita chose to do. Nonetheless, some view relocation as a viable option and follow the lead of fictional character Jean Valjean in the Broadway performance of Les Miserables, which was made even more popular by its 2012 screenplay.

In 1815, Jean Valjean is granted parole by prison guard Javert following a nineteen-year sentence for stealing a loaf of bread. Unfortunately, the stigma of being an ex-convict precludes him from obtaining employment or any town's acceptance until the Bishop of Digne offers him a place to stay. Desperate, Valjean steals the bishop's silver during the night and finds himself once again in the hands of the authorities. Yet again, the bishop comes to Valjean's rescue, telling the authorities that he gave the silver to Valjean as a gift; the thief's release was secured.

Valjean, in light of the bishop's extraordinary show of grace, opts to break his parole by relocating to the town of Montreuil-sur-Mer under a new identity as both the mayor and a factory owner, but irony ensues when he finds that Javert has been assigned as the town's new chief of police. From their very first meeting, Javert recognizes something familiar about Valjean but is unable to determine what. As the story proceeds, evidence continues to convince Javert of Valjean's true identity.

Sometime later, the two men learn that a man believed to be Valjean has been arrested. Overwhelmed by the idea of an innocent man imprisoned for his actions, Valjean reveals his true identity. In the summarized version of the story provided here, Valjean and police chief Javert scuffle, yet Valjean inevitably escapes Javert's grasp. The reality for Jean Valjean is that, although he has experienced a life change and reinvented himself (elsewhere), he has never dealt with and consequently never truly escaped his past.

Jean Valjean, although a fictional character, exhibits behaviors that resonate with the relationship paradox of whether to reinvent locally or elsewhere. He was forced to live his life in fear of his past relationship infractions, always wondering when they would 'find' him. Valjean, whether he realized it or not, was being haunted by the missing reconciliation between those he had wronged and himself.

It is an inescapable challenge to visit relationships, past and present, against whom you have infracted. Embarrassment of the person that you were and the shame for the behaviors that you once exhibited form the emotional landscape that comes with a greater awareness of self. Grace offers the realization that there is an expansive distance between where you have been and where you ought to be, but it does so with the hope for a future carved by restoration and wholeness. Within the biblical model (Appendix A-6), Jesus places preeminence on reconciliation above other activities; in essence, attempts must be made to rebuild that which has been broken. Yes, attempting to make amends is a non-negotiable, even if it places you as the offender or offended in an undesirable social situation.

In chapter 4, we opened the discussion on the requirements of forgiveness in a relationship. Inasmuch as forgiveness is to be offered unconditionally and perpetually, grace demands legitimate attempts toward reconciliation. Jean Valjean failed to live a life of peace when he relocated to Montreuil-sur-Mer because he never sought reconciliation in past relationships despite his vow to alter the course of his future.

The fictional protagonist Valjean perpetuates a grave misconception held by many who claim internal change by grace–that the actual change sufficiently satisfies all prescribed reconciliatory activities. This assumption is flawed, as it does not solve for states of relationship strain (S) in existing relationships and breaches of the tolerance threshold (T) in broken relationships. Reconciliation with the recipients of one's past infractions, as well as reconciliation with the creator of the law infracted upon (God), are both demands of grace.

In chapter 5, we opened the discussion to the stabilization of relationship equity and addressed the manner in which we attempt to reinvent self. Now, as we proceed into chapter 6, we will explore the many applications of relationship equity.

6

APPLICATIONS OF EQUITY

Understanding the implied applications of the relation equation is crucial for a number of reasons, regardless of whether the focus is on internalization or instruction. Personal application, facilitation, and communication of relationship equity are practical outlets through which the relation equation theory can function.

PERSONAL APPLICATION

Internally Focused–Uncovering the internalized benefits of the relation equation has been the majority of our journey thus far. Developing an understanding of how we interact with others is critical to our development as leaders and more importantly as inherently compassionate people. The entirety of our past is relevant to understanding how we acquire and maintain relationships and is always a reflection of our own nurturing. In essence, we are going to build relationships in the same way that we were shown by others around us at a young age to build them. There is an old adage that says the way in which a man has been raised to behave toward his mother now is a good indicator of how that man will treat a woman in a future romantic relationship. Whether or not this theory is based on scientific data is irrelevant, as it has received enough notoriety from pure observation to be validated. Of course, should we wish to break free from potentially destructive behaviors, we must be intentional about both the way in which we acquire and the way in which we use relationship equity.

The power and influence of "nurture" has been grossly underestimated in an effort to validate the significance of "nature." We have become so entangled in pursuits of finding and offering validation for every known lifestyle choice that nurture has lost much of its influence to nature. This argument is undoubtedly controversial in contemporary society and will be unpalatable for some readers.

Our propensity is to dispose of relationship after relationship and to blame the failure on the other individual's incompatibility with 'me' as a person. As a pastor, I have facilitated more counseling sessions than I would care to recall with individual after individual who declares his/her refusal to change for anyone. We cling stubbornly to Popeye's "I y'am what I y'am" life philosophy of pseudo self-actualization rather than maintaining an open dialogue with those whom we have engaged in relationship. Once our disposition mirrors Popeye's, we no longer exchange equity out of love; we do so out of pride and self-gain.

Prematurely, we move to blame the 'nature' of the other participants involved in a relationship instead of taking a closer look at the flawed points of our own 'nurtured' behaviors. Note that this does not give a participant license to outright blame the person(s) responsible for his/her upbringing; it simply establishes that the external stimuli an individual has been exposed to play a significant role in the treatment of that person's relationships.

Worldview has much to do with relationship management. The things that shaped your worldview may not be naturally placing you on a trajectory of healthy relationships. As a result, if your relationships are consistently unsuccessful, "they" may not be the problem; "you" may.

Externally Focused–Once we have internalized the benefits of relationship equity, our outlook on and approach to relationships ought to change for the better. Moving forward, we are adequately poised to apply those benefits to both existing as well as new relationships. In either case, theory must meet practice; and the evidence should be healthier exchanges of equity.

In chapter 7, the conversation will turn to the motives driving exchanges of equity, although for our present purposes we will indicate that motives of an impure or ulterior origin do not fall into the paradigm of healthy exchanges of relationship equity. Having stated such, the relationships already in progress ought to benefit from new efforts to create equity in an appropriate manner. The chapter 5 stabilizing equity discussion revealed two unique reinvention-of-self scenarios in which internal change had transpired. We will not revisit the entirety of that discussion, but instead mention a couple of additional caveats; primarily, awareness that it may be difficult for people to accept the fact that you have changed internally.

Once the introduction barriers have been overcome and the relationship is in progress, conscious efforts can be made in new relationships to not repeat the mistakes of former ones; this can be achieved by intentionally applying the relation equation. As a pastor, one of the most noticeable pitfalls is an individual who has not addressed and made subsequent effort to correct the poor relationship practices of the past. Instead, he/she continues in the next relationship with the same behavior that destroyed the prior relationship(s), whether engaged with the same participant as before or engaged with a new one.

A few years ago a young woman whom I knew through my corporate job asked me to perform her wedding and I quickly agreed to the job contingent upon Emma and Matt's completing my prescribed premarital counseling. It didn't take long to discover that the volatile cocktail of Matt's drug use and extreme jealousy, which had prevented them from marrying at an earlier date, were still major barriers in this relationship. The couple parented a well-adjusted little girl and had taken up residence together now for a few years, but had yet to further commit.

Emma and Matt were the quintessential on-again/off-again couple, who likely stayed together as long as they did because of their little girl. The indecisive two made a regular habit of breaking-up and getting back together, doing so without resolving any of the issues that caused them to break up in the first place. The marriage proposal served to be no different from any other period in their relationship together, as they broke up before the counseling was complete.

FACILITATING THE PROCESS

Relationship equity is essential to opening the lines of communication with those with whom you are attempting to communicate. Each argument presented in a relationship that stands contrary to a participant's point of view will require a use of equity proportionate to the difference between the viewpoint and the recipient's worldview. Conveying controversial or unpalatable messages will require hefty withdrawals of relationship equity, depending upon rebuttals or rebuffs. Thus, the presence of sufficient relationship equity creates provision to be heard by the other participant in the relationship.

Given instances where the result of spent equity, through expression of a point of view, is a net loss, the relationship can still be maintained if the tolerance threshold (T) has not been breached. To elaborate, the first withdrawal of equity was used for the purposes of being heard and was unsuccessful; this is why you waited until you had ample relationship equity before making your petition. Although the relationship may now have less equity, it is not destroyed. If the point of view is truly worth expressing, your job now is to rebuild lost equity, potentially circle back, and attempt the conversation again.

If the result of spent equity is positive, celebrate the increase in relationship equity. Only a passive pessimist assumes that every outcome of risking relationship equity for the purpose of conveying a viewpoint will yield negative results. If the outcome of the petition is positive, it could result in a significant increase in relationship equity, thereby becoming a new shared experience.

One of the greatest leadership missteps is a propensity to verbally push a viewpoint, or agenda, onto a person with whom a leader has failed to build sufficient equity. In the biblical model, Jesus focused on cultivating relationships in addition to verbally conveying truth. Throughout His earthly ministry, He focused greatly on building equity by caring for the most basic needs of people.

In a poignant passage of scripture (Appendix A-7), Jesus guides one of His closest disciples, Peter, to care for people as a result of a deeply rooted love for Him (Jesus) as well as a love for the people for whom He was charged to care. In this interaction, Jesus thrice asks Peter if he loves Him. On Peter's first and third inquiries, Jesus requests that Peter takes His sheep to pasture. On Peter's second inquiry, Jesus reveals that Peter is to become a guardian over His sheep. Jesus presents this caveat of leadership: There is no way to serve in the capacity of mentor without first developing relationship.

The ability to communicate the principles of the relation equation is critical to the mentoring process; thus, the mentoring process is predicated on an ability to build relationships. A primary passage within the biblical text that communicates the duty to mentor–or in the context of Christian life, disciple–is given in Jesus' final words on Earth. At its very essence, the Great Commission (Appendix A-8) demands discipleship; and discipleship is predicated on relationship.

Discipleship demands a mentor-mentee relationship based on maturity of faith that disregards many traditional theories. It speaks to the qualifier in mentor-mentee relationships as maturity in faith as opposed to maturity in age. Regardless of religious inclination, the premise that the young can offer instruction to his/her elders is revolutionary in many worldview contexts.

Presently, I serve as an adjunct professor of management in the school of business and leadership at a local university. The specific program that I teach classes for offers evening classes to accommodate working professionals who are attempting to complete their unfinished bachelor's degrees from other colleges and universities. As a man of thirty-three, I am privileged to serve a wide range of students aging from those in their mid-twenties to those quickly closing in on retirement; more times than not, the student's age exceeds my own. It is not as though this type of mentoring relationship comes without its share of challenges; I typically do get a few looks of uncertainty on students' faces the first night of class. Even so, the student's receptivity quickly changes when they realize that I have insights of potential value to contribute to their worldview.

In the Apostle Paul's address (Appendix A-9) to Timothy, he (1) illustrates himself as Timothy's mentor, instructing Timothy on proper behavior and (2) breaks the paradigm of age being a qualifier in mentor-mentee relationships as Paul charges Timothy to mentor others. Paul, the mentor, was urging Timothy to act in a manner that would leave no one room to discount him because of his young age. In fact, the language that Paul uses to instruct Timothy on what to do is fitting to the mandate. He uses the Greek 'typos,' or a figure formed by impression, in order to describe Timothy's duty to exemplify the proper behavior before those to whom he is charged to lead. Furthermore, to ensure that Timothy remains true to the example that he is charged with setting, Paul specifically instructs him to set an example in "logos" (word and speech), in "anastrophe" (conduct or manner of living), in "agape" (unrelenting love mirroring that of God's), in "pistis" (conviction and belief), and in "hagneia" (purity). In essence, Paul delivers a tall order for Timothy to fill.

In chapter 6, we opened the discussion to the applications of relationship equity, be it applied personally or through instruction. Now, as we proceed into chapter 7, we will explore the motives behind the pursuit of relationship equity.

7

DRIVE FOR RESULTS

MOTIVES

Since we have now identified/defined what relationship equity is, our understanding of relationship equity must be more than discussion of theory; it should be intentional practice. However, intentional takes many forms, all of which are dependent upon motive. There is a poignant passage within the biblical text (Appendix A-10) that speaks to the relationship between motive and action. When Jesus spoke about wrongdoing–and He did so on multiple occasions–He equated the thought of wrongdoing with the act of wrongdoing. The pervasive argument of The Relation Equation is that the motive driving our desire to build relationship equity is the most important element in the model. Refer to US law for affirmation that we have accepted the significance of intentionality as a society; consider the difference between crimes such as (1) vehicular homicide as the direct result of drunk-driving and (2) pre-meditated murder. If intentional motives are discovered, the penalty for the infraction is often more severe.

Hopefully, the arguments presented thus far should lead us to an assumption of this basic construct: The motive for our investment in a relationship must be love. Jesus offers this directive (Appendix A-11) with a great degree of clarity as He affirms the primacy of love. When provoked to offer preference to one law over the others in an overtly legalistic society (yes, He was being trapped by the teachers of the law), Jesus chose to elevate the supremacy of love to first God and then, as a result, everyone else. The commandments relating to murder, adultery, theft, altering truth, and jealousy are all potential infractions against a relationship that can be avoided by approaching the relationship with perfect love. Granted we can never live perfect, infraction-free lives; but we can strive for pure motives by rooting them in an agape kind of love. Once again from the biblical text, Matthew chooses to use "agape" to indicate the type of Godly love that we are to mirror in our relationships: a love so deep that it stretches beyond action or emotion and reaches to motive. Motive is the one thing that we cannot escape–we will always answer to and for the intentions of our heart.

The relation equation does not account for an aggregate of what deeds, good or bad, a relationship participant banks. An early 2000s television sitcom offered a comedic display of this behavior, wherein an aloof husband (Jeff) kept a record of all the infractions against the relationship made by his wife (Audrey), so as to be able to remind her when he did something wrong that he didn't get mad at her over one of those things. Of course, she eventually became aware of the bank; and the action of keeping such an account in and of itself became an infraction against the relationship. True love (Appendix A-12) does not keep a record of wrongs. Unlike our friend Jeff, who felt as though he needed a record of Audrey's infractions so as to avoid confrontation with her when he infracted against the relationship, our mandate is to perpetually offer forgiveness. We continue doing so motivated by love for God, fellow man, and out of gratefulness that we have been forgiven more than we could ever forgive.

DESPITE UNSPOKEN RESULTS

Verbal validation of a successful relationship may never overtly be offered to participants searching for it. The very status of a relationship may be in question when some form of affirmation is unknown; this is no mystery or new revelation. Counselors have likely spent more time than they would care to admit offering comfort and logic to participants in the relationship experience who fail to receive the validation they are forever seeking out, be it hearing words of extravagant love or simple appreciation.

The functionality of a relationship depends upon the presence of love. Although there are those in this life who consistently offer verbal affirmation of how they view the trajectory of a relationship, some participants in the experience prefer to leave such sentiments unspoken. Still, for he/she who chooses to leave affirmation of his/her love for another unspoken, uncertainty can surround the relationship if love isn't adequately expressed through other means.

Consider many fathers of the twentieth century. Verbally expressing the words "I love you" to their wife and kids wasn't necessarily a manly thing to do, so many men chose not to do so. Did this somehow mean that these fathers didn't love their families? Quite the contrary; in many cases they worked harder to provide for their loved ones than generations before them or after. Even so, expressing love for another is most effectively done when word (verbalizing "I love you") and deed (loving through actions) are coupled together.

Another example comes from observations at the non-profit mentioned in the Preface, Agape. The business model was designed to engage the community through a viable retail operation that fit into the landscape of the neighborhood, although our primary objective was to build meaningful relationships with our neighbors. In fact, the board of directors, including me, lived in the community for one year prior to opening the gallery space. We shopped there, ate there, and socialized there because we had a deep love for the existing culture; so, when it was time to rent the space and hang art on the wall, we were not completely unknown.

In any entrepreneurial venture, it is natural to evaluate the success of the unique endeavor on a micro level even if the individual patterns more appropriately call for an evaluation on the macro level. Take, for example, winter activities. As for Agape, the gallery was not the only affected business during harsh winters; the community as a whole suffered from the cold and snow. When the economy slowed, the industry creating and selling art began to suffer, not just Agape. Thus, it is important to understand that success, while not always visible, may be masked by forces beyond an individual person's control. Nevertheless, it is easy to allow the discouragement of a couple poorly attended evenings overshadow the seemingly minor inroads that were made in spite of adverse conditions.

Minor inroads are the true victory stories of relationship equity. Take, for example, the account of a man named Stan, a veteran of the United States Navy from the Vietnam conflict. Stan is visibly disabled and cannot drive, so he uses the transportation that creator God gave him–legs–to walk up the hill to the mini mart every day for a six pack of light beer. His trek would regularly take him past the front entrance of our six hundred square foot gallery space on Literary Road, which is where our paths met without the bias of coincidence. We would invite Stan to come inside the gallery and sit down, as it was roughly the halfway point between his apartment and the mini mart. Usually, by this point in his trek, he was out of breath anyway. He would stay, and we would talk. Stan is likely not the type of fellow whom the designer-label patron in our well-to-do neighborhood would be eager to engage, for he wore old clothes with many rips and snags, rarely shaved, and was missing a significant number of front teeth. This guy probably did not have much in common with the wealthy patrons waiting for their table at one of the neighborhood's nationally known restaurants.

There was something pure about the relationship we built with Stan, and I do not believe that the gallery's relocation concludes the story of our relationship with him. An investment was made in a relationship that became especially evident on our final day in the neighborhood: Stan wished us well and helped load furniture and fixtures into the moving truck.

In chapter 7, we began discussing the motives behind the pursuit of relationship equity. Now, as we proceed into chapter 8, we will explore the types of relationships that can prove to be toxic.

8

TRANSACTIONAL RELATIONSHIPS

TOXICITY

To this point, we have focused our attention primarily on the elements of building healthy relationships; however, there are relationships that are both unhealthy and not beneficial in which to continue engaging. The conversation around motive requires that we address transactional relationships and their inevitable pitfalls. Transactional relationships are either formed or deeply invested in with the intention of acquiring a personal benefit or gain.

Star Struck–It is a normative part of the human condition to become a bit star-struck from time to time. Whether the admiration is directed at a famed musician, favorite actor/actress, or renowned artist, we enjoy meeting those individuals who have contributed to the masses. As a result, individuals seek out relationships with, or remain engaged in relationships with, persons of notoriety or fame. This process is not to be confused with granted equity through association as was discussed in chapter 3. Star struck stands separate because of the difference in motives.

When I think of this particular scenario, star-struck groupies immediately come to mind. Often these relationships are highly invested in by the participant who has the meager social status and shallowly invested in by the participant with the more pronounced social status. Take, for example, the character of Annie Wilkes in the 1990 film entitled "Misery." Wilkes was so enamored with the authorship of writer Paul Sheldon that she essentially kidnapped him, forcing him to write against his wishes. The story is, of course, much more elaborate than described here. Nonetheless, she was a classic example of a star-struck individual who was far more vested in a relationship with him than he was with her.

Gold Digger–A prevalent form of the transactional relationship is that of the gold digger, an individual who invests significant time and effort into acquiring the resources of another. These relationships are superficial at best, oftentimes leaving one party (the resource holder) in the dark about the true intentions of the other party (the resource taker). This relationship type is by no means limited to that of a wealthy, elderly male and a vibrant young woman of twenty-one; but that is likely the first thought coming to mind. The implications of "gold digger" stretch to any relationship in which resource acquisition has replaced love as a motive–fully or in part.

One of my pet-peeves fit the "gold digger" model nicely. I subscribe to a traditional manner of dating where the man escorts the woman from her door or wherever else they arrange to meet, sees her to her door at the end of the evening, and pays for dinner. Primary among those activities is picking up the bill; it is a non-negotiable. However, I appreciate it greatly when the woman offers to do so, even though I will not accept her offer. No man wants to feel as though a date is merely an excuse for a free meal, and no person wants to feel as though a transaction has taken place.

Financially Fearful–Resource drivers in relationships are not exclusive to the gold-digger scenario. Some remain engaged in relationships with persons for the purposes of workplace stability. I would estimate that anyone who has performed as an employee of a company has at some point experienced and tolerated subpar behavior from another individual in the workplace, be it from a superior or coworker. There are severely unpalatable circumstances, such as an individual tolerating sexual harassment, that are tolerated because the infracted upon individual needs the job and feels as though addressing the issue will jeopardize that. At this point, the tolerance threshold (T) has been breached, and the interaction between the participants has become purely transactional.

Although some relationships may have started out with genuinely pure intentions, the choice to remain in a transactional relationship for the purpose of gain is a conscious one–and a poor one, at that. Once it becomes apparent that the relationship has become toxic, it no longer follows the rules of the relation equation. Should the participant on the receiving end of the abuse, whether it be physical or verbal, remain in the relationship, it should be noted that he/she is not exercising a socially normative valuation process for the relationship. Therefore, the participant tolerating the abuse has grossly misplaced the tolerance threshold (T).

A frequently disclosed reason for the tolerance of abuse is a participant's inability to afford living on his/her own or the belief that that he/she cannot do so. This point is not exclusively associated with monetary motives, as an individual may have bought into the premise that no one else would ever love him/her. Take, for example, the story of a young woman whom we will call Janice. Janice has been in a relationship with her high-school boyfriend for the past six years, and they have a four-year-old son together. Despite the constant verbal (and occasional physical) abuse that her boyfriend doles out to her, she believes that there are insufficient resources to move out of the house. Instead, she numbs herself to the barrage of socially condemned abuses. It is at this point that the self-worth of Janice has been diminished. Janice now believes that not only does she hold insufficient resources to discontinue the toxic relationship, but she is incapable of acquiring the love of another person.

Controlled–It was not until Agape hosted a Human Trafficking awareness month that I began to more acutely understand the impact of diminishing self-worth upon control in a relationship.

It is the staunch assertion of this text that a controlling relationship of any form is toxic and unsolvable by means of the relation equation. Individuals seek out relationships, or remain engaged in them, to get something below cost. A prime example of this is compensation for sex, more accurately labeled human-trafficking activities. This text takes the unwavering stance that there is no moral justification for participants to partake in these activities, even in circumstances where they are considered legally allowable. Up to this point, we have built upon the premise that the only acceptable motive for relationship is love; thus, there is no possible way that compensation for a sexual activity could ever be sufficient enough to morally justify the damaging transactional nature of the activity.

In chapter 8, we opened the discussion to transactional relationships and the danger of their toxicity. Now, as we proceed into chapter 9, we finish the text by facing this inevitable part of many existing and potential relationships: rejection.

9

REJECTION

IMPOSSIBLE INTRODUCTIONS

This text is not an answer to creating relationships, as it assumes that individuals are actively participating in at least one relationship. The relation equation cannot solve for introductions and is therefore void of any strategy for meeting people. As a result, the principles mentioned in this text are designed to help us become more intentional about the way we build relationships already in progress, not to be used as tools to manipulate an individual into participating in a relationship with us.

In the 2005 film entitled Hitch, a suave dating consultant makes his living by helping average men meet, date, and develop romantic relationships with women whom they likely would otherwise be unable to connect with if left to their own devices. The film depicted multiple love stories that were attributed to the coaching of one Alex "Hitch" Hitchens. All seemed well until the paparazzi, one of which ironically had become Hitch's personal love interest, revealed the identity of this illusive date-doctor. When exposed, the women involved found the deed deceitful and manipulative.

Hitch's assumption that relationships could be formulaically created and sustained by the same means was incorrect. Relationships that begin with an altered version of truth must continue with that same reality to survive. However, the longer the lie is perpetuated, the more infractions are occurring against any positive equity available. This illustration provides this far-reaching principle: Even if the altered truth is shielding the infracted person from a minor reality, he/she is still being infracted upon through the perpetuation of a lie.

STALLED EQUITY

There are times when an exchange of relationship equity ceases from all participants involved in a relationship. As happens in a combustion motor, the result of stalling is the loss of functionality. A stalled relationship is one in which all active participants have simultaneously ceased any further investment. Since the investing stopped, despite the lack of any new infractions against the relationship, the potential value will simply approach zero as interest (investment) in the relationship ceases to exist.

RELATIONALLY REJECTED

We have established that the relation equation does not offer assistance with introductions; however, the nuances of rejection are as equally applicable to existing relationships as they are to the introductions. A parable (Appendix A-13) told by Jesus foreshadows this occurrence. The context of the story is that some of His disciples are searching within a town for a home that would openly receive them as guests. Should they be received well, the occupants of the home were greeted with peace; however, if the disciples were rejected, they were to retract their presence and initial offering of peace. This passage of Scripture is valuable to our study of rejection because it illustrates the rejection of an individual's mere presence before words are uttered as well as rejection that occurs after a relationship has begun.

Although it is not an entirely palatable assertion, there is a segment of the population with which a given individual will be unable to connect. This is true to the reality that, for whatever reason, there will be people groups with whom an individual will never participate in a relationship. Proceeding forward in this text, we will refer to these reasons for non-participation as barriers.

Barriers to forming relationships (impossible introductions) or barriers to maintaining them (stalled equity) occur in various forms. The most obvious barrier is a physical one or that pertaining to geographic location. Although technology has closed the communication gap when the geographical barrier is expansive, relationship participants still require physical interaction. This is why long-distance relationships often fail, even ones that have been stable for a long period of time prior to the geographic separation. There are, of course, an abundance of superficial barriers as well. For example, an individual's physical appearance may preclude him/her from entering into a dating relationship with someone who has an aversion to a particular type. Sometimes barriers can be as simple as unrelatable demographic attributes such as cultural practices or mores, religion, nationality, race, color, sex, or sexual orientation. In any case, rejection is an unavoidable part of the human experience.

In chapter 9, we completed our discussion on relationships by addressing rejection. In the pages to come, we will offer some final thoughts on the universal applicability of the relation equation.

FINAL THOUGHTS

The introduction to the text provides some insight into process-ing a relationship through an unlikely paradigm. As an author, speaker, teacher, and pastor, my goal has consistently been to find ways for people to understand challenging or abstract principles through already familiar paradigms. The Relation Equation was designed to expose both the subversively held and overtly under-stood nuances of relationships and to view them through the lens of a modified formula for equity.

We have adopted an understanding that people are tangible because we have the ability to connect with one another physically, but relationships do not share that attribute. Blindly believing that motives and relationship equity exchanges are explainable by a physical descriptive is irresponsible, regardless of whether or not you share my Christian worldview. I would challenge the critic to build a paradigm that defines relationships materially.

To say the least, mapping relationships is a subjective pro-cess, thus using the paradigm of equity provides some sense of substantive objectivity to evaluating the quality of a relationship. In context, the very attempt to measure a relationship feels nearly reminiscent of King Solomon's repetition of 'a chasing after the wind' found throughout the Old Testament account of Ecclesias-tes. Nonetheless, without the authority to apply psychological or sociological theory to the intangible and immeasurable activity of relationship, this project led to equity as a construct to explain the exchanges occurring between people.

I hope by this point that you feel as though you have been introduced to more than abstract theory or empty conjecture but have been able to view your own relationships through the paradigm of equity. If you allow them to be, the implications of The Relation Equation are broad and far reaching, answering questions within the deepest, darkest parts of our relationship challenges.

Appendix A

BIBLICAL REFERENCE

APPENDIX A-1

"My command is this: Love each other as I have loved you. Greater love has no one than this that he lay down his life for his friends." (John 15:12–13 New International Version)

APPENDIX A-2

"For I was hungry and you gave me something to eat, I was thirsty and you gave me something to drink, I was a stranger and you invited me in, I needed clothes and you clothed me, I was sick and you looked after me, I was in prison and you came to visit me.' "Then the righteous will answer him, 'Lord, when did we see you hungry and feed you, or thirsty and give you something to drink? When did we see you a stranger and invite you in, or needing clothes and clothe you? When did we see you sick or in prison and go to visit you?' "The King will reply, 'I tell you the truth, whatever you did for one of the least of these brothers of mine, you did for me.'" (Matthew 25:35–40 New International Version)

Appendix A

APPENDIX A-3

"Children, obey your parents in the Lord, for this is right. "Honor your father and mother"—which is the first commandment with a promise—"that it may go well with you and that you may enjoy long life on the earth." Fathers, do not exasperate your children; instead, bring them up in the training and instruction of the Lord." (Ephesians 6:1–4 New International Version)

APPENDIX A-4

"Submit to one another out of reverence for Christ. Wives, submit to your husbands as to the Lord. For the husband is the head of the wife as Christ is the head of the church, his body, of which he is the Savior. Now as the church submits to Christ, so also wives should submit to their husbands in everything. Husbands, love your wives, just as Christ loved the church and gave himself up for her." (Ephesians 5:21–25 New International Version)

APPENDIX A-5

"Then Peter came to Jesus and asked, "Lord, how many times shall I forgive my brother when he sins against me? Up to seven times?" Jesus answered, "I tell you, not seven times, but seventy-seven times. "Therefore, the kingdom of heaven is like a king who wanted to settle accounts with his servants. As he began the settlement, a man who owed him ten thousand talents was brought to him. Since he was not able to pay, the master ordered that he and his wife and his children and all that he had be sold to repay the debt. The servant fell on his knees before him. 'Be patient with me,' he begged, 'and I will pay back everything.' The servant's master took pity on him, canceled the debt and let him go. "But when that servant went out, he found one of his fellow servants who owed him a hundred denarii. He grabbed him and began to choke him. 'Pay back what you owe me!' he demanded. "His fellow servant fell to his knees and begged him, 'Be patient with me, and I will pay you back.' "But he refused. Instead, he went off and had the man thrown into prison until he could pay the debt. When the other servants saw what had happened, they were greatly distressed and went and told their master everything that had happened. "Then the master called the servant in. 'You wicked servant,' he said, 'I canceled all that debt of yours because you begged me to. Shouldn't you have had mercy on your fellow servant just as I had on you?' In anger his master turned him over to the jailers to be tortured, until he should pay back all he owed. "This is how my heavenly Father will treat each of you unless you forgive your brother from your heart." (Matthew 18:21–35 New International Version)

APPENDIX A-6

"If you are offering your gift at the altar and there remember that your brother has something against you, leave your gift there in front of the altar. First go and be reconciled to your brother; then come and offer your gift." (Matthew 5:23–24 New International Version)

APPENDIX A-7

When they had finished eating, Jesus said to Simon Peter, "Simon son of John, do you truly love me more than these?" "Yes, Lord," he said, "you know that I love you." Jesus said, "Feed my lambs." Again Jesus said, "Simon son of John, do you truly love me?" He answered, "Yes, Lord, you know that I love you." Jesus said, "Take care of my sheep." The third time he said to him, "Simon son of John, do you love me?" Peter was hurt because Jesus asked him the third time, "Do you love me?" He said, "Lord, you know all things; you know that I love you." Jesus said, "Feed my sheep." (John 21:15–17 New International Version)

APPENDIX A-8

"Then Jesus came to them and said, "All authority in heaven and on earth has been given to me. Therefore go and make disciples of all nations, baptizing them in the name of the Father and of the Son and of the Holy Spirit, and teaching them to obey everything I have commanded you. And surely I am with you always, to the very end of the age." (Matthew 28:18–20 New International Version)

APPENDIX A-9

"Don't let anyone look down on you because you are young, but set an example for the believers in speech, in life, in love, in faith and in purity." (1 Timothy 4:12 New International Version)

APPENDIX A-10

"You have heard that it was said to the people long ago, 'Do not murder, and anyone who murders will be subject to judgment.' But I tell you that anyone who is angry with his brother will be subject to judgment. Again, anyone who says to his brother, 'Raca, 'is answerable to the Sanhedrin. But anyone who says, 'You fool!' will be in danger of the fire of hell." (Matthew 5:21–22 New International Version)

APPENDIX A-11

"Hearing that Jesus had silenced the Sadducees, the Pharisees got together. One of them, an expert in the law, tested him with this question: "Teacher, which is the greatest commandment in the Law?" Jesus replied: "'Love the Lord your God with all your heart and with all your soul and with all your mind.' This is the first and greatest commandment. And the second is like it: 'Love your neighbor as yourself.' All the Law and the Prophets hang on these two commandments." (Matthew 22:34–40 New International Version)

APPENDIX A-12

"Love is patient, love is kind. It does not envy, it does not boast, it is not proud. It is not rude, it is not self-seeking, it is not easily angered, it keeps no record of wrongs." (1 Corinthians 13:4–5 New International Version)

APPENDIX A-13

"As you enter the home, give it your greeting. If the home is deserving, let your peace rest on it; if it is not, let your peace return to you. If anyone will not welcome you or listen to your words, shake the dust off your feet when you leave that home or town." (Matthew 10:12–14 New International Version)

APPENDIX B

EQUATIONS

APPENDIX B-1

E=P(T)-S

Equity will always be less than the potential value. (E<P)

Equity will always be less than the tolerance threshold. (E<T)

Tolerance threshold will always be less than, and dependent upon the potential value, since the tolerance threshold can only equal the potential value if perfect love was attainable in a relationship. (T<P)

Relationship strain will always be less than the tolerance threshold. (S<T)

Relationship strain will always be less than the potential value. (S<P)

APPENDIX B-2

E(John)=P(T(Jane))-S

E(Jane)=P(T(John))-S

ABOUT THE AUTHOR

Stephen graduated with a Master of Business Administration from Bluffton University, a Master of Arts in Theological Studies from the Assemblies of God Theological Seminary and a Bachelor of Science from Lake Erie College. He serves as the Executive Director of Agape Inc., and has assembled relationally relevant experience through pastoral appointments, employment at premier financial institutions, and an Adjunct Professor role within the School of Business and Leadership at Malone University in Canton, Ohio.

www.ingramcontent.com/pod-product-compliance
Lightning Source LLC
Chambersburg PA
CBHW071105090426
42737CB00013B/2493